Posh Nosh

RECIPES FROM CELEBRITIES

Dedication

Sister Aloysius and Father Tom Mulherran for their inspiration and to all the care team of Francis House.

FRANCIS HOUSE
CHILDREN'S HOSPICE

Foreword

by Raymond Blanc

Posh Nosh is a fun cook book, a collaboration of recipes, thoughts and words from the rich and famous. The inspiration for the book has been Francis House Children's Hospice's 10th Birthday. As our north-west children's hospice, it offers help and respite care to children with a short life expectancy. I can't think of a more worthy cause to motivate such an entertaining project.

Francis House is a haven of warmth, reassurance and support and the contributors to Posh Nosh reflect this beautifully. Each one has suggested a recipe that means a great deal to them personally – from rice crispies to chairman's pudding!

As you browse through Posh Nosh, please spare a thought for the children and families that are dependent upon Francis House.

Posh Nosh

First published in Great Britain in 2001
for
Francis House Children's Hospice
Rainbow Family Trust
Charity Reg. No. 328659
Manchester

ISBN: 0-9541499-0-4

Designed and printed in Great Britain
by Lithaprint Limited, Stockport.

These recipes have been given in good faith by the celebrities to support this worthy cause. Whilst every effort has been made, none of those concerned with the compilation of this book may be held responsible in any way for errors or omissions contained herein.

Acknowledgments

Carole, Judy and Millie are hugely indebted to all the individuals and celebrities that have contributed to this book. They are busy people who have given generously of their time in support of Francis House Children's Hospice - without their help and encouragement 'Posh Nosh' would never have been produced.

To Raymond Blanc for his kindness in supplying us with the Foreword and the book launch in Manchester.

To Tony, Neil and staff of Lithaprint, Stockport who were crucial to the final product.

To Booths Supermarkets, especially Michael Lough, who initiated sales through their stores.

Few people accurately weigh or measure quantities, therefore take care with the mix of metric and imperial measurements.

Contributors

Bombay Toast

GEORGE ALAGIAH

This is now a favourite with my two sons. I do it for a weekend breakfast. I think people in Britain know it as 'French Toast', but when I grew up, first in Sri Lanka and then Ghana, my mum always called it Bombay Toast. Don't ask me why!

4 eggs
six slices white bread
dark muscovado sugar
milk
butter
cinnamon powder

Put the eggs and milk into a bowl and beat thoroughly. Soak the bread slices, two at a time, in the beaten egg and milk. Fry in butter till the bread is lightly browned on both sides. Keep warm while you fry the rest of the bread then sprinkle with the cinnamon and dark sugar to taste.

A variation on this, eaten in Sri Lanka: add chopped green chillies into egg and eat as a savoury - not for the faint-hearted!

You may be interested to know that my mother used to use something called jaggeri instead of brown sugar. This was a molasses like sugar from the palmera palms that grow so abundantly in Sri Lanka.

Chairman's Pudding

MOHAMMAD AL FAYED

Serves 4-6

1 pint milk (full fat or semi-skimmed)
26g (1oz) caster sugar
2 eggs (size 2)
70g (2 1/2 oz) butter
1 pint whipping cream
4 egg yolks (size 2)
100g (3 1/2 oz) sultanas
small loaf of white bread, medium sliced (approx. 16 slices)

Pour the milk and cream into a pan and bring to the boil. Whisk egg yolks, eggs and caster sugar. Add hot milk and cream mixture and blend. Strain into a bowl. Sprinkle half the sultanas into the bottom of a medium sized ovenproof dish. Remove crusts from bread slices and cut into diagonal quarters. Arrange diagonal quarters in the dish, overlapping each layer until the dish is filled, placing small cubes of butter on the bread. Pour egg mixture over the bread and sprinkle with remaining sultanas.

Place in deep baking tin half filled with warm water. Cook in the oven at 150°C/300°F/gas mark 2 for approx. 50 minutes or until golden brown.

Raspberry Sauce
Puree and sieve 200g (7oz) fresh raspberries. Bring to the boil 75g (3oz) sugar and 75ml (2 1/2 fl oz) red burgundy with a slice of lemon rind. Add raspberry puree and reduce for about 3-4 minutes.

Apricot Sauce
Blanch, skin and stone 250g (9oz) of ripe apricots. Puree in a blender with 7 tablespoons of sugar syrup (boil equal amounts of water and sugar for 3-4 minutes). Stir in 2 teaspoons of fresh lime juice.

These sauces can be served warm or cold.

When serving, pour the raspberry sauce on to the plate, surround it with the apricot sauce and place a portion of pudding on top. If you are intent on going entirely over the top, a scoop of frozen yoghurt on the side will certainly do the trick.

Penne al Pollo Picante

FRANK ALLEN

Serves 4

olive oil
1 small onion, peeled and chopped (flakes rather than diced)
2 red chillies, de-seeded and chopped
 or tablespoon dried chopped chillies (adjust to taste)
half pound penne pasta (packet or fresh)
1 pre-cooked chicken
2oz mushrooms, sliced
half pint chicken stock (fresh or stock cubes)
 or Mexican stock cubes for more spicy taste

Remove flesh of chicken from bones by hand and roughly tear into bite size pieces rather than cut.

Heat 2 tablespooons of oil in saucepan and add onion till transparent. Add sliced mushrooms and gently stir till brown. Add chillies. Pour in half the stock and bring to simmering point. Add chicken pieces and continue to simmer, adding more stock depending on consistency. Liquid should have some body, but not too thick. If too thick, add more stock. If thin, mix 2 teaspoons of cornflour with 2 tablespoons of milk and add gradually till required thickness is reached. Do not add all at once and only add as much as is needed. Simmer for approx. 20 minutes.

Meanwhile, place penne in lightly salted water which has been brought to the boil and cook for ten minutes, stirring occasionally.

Drain and divide into portions. Pour over chicken mixture. Best served with warmed ciabatta bread.

The liquid can be adjusted to taste by adding or removing spices of your choice or adding tomatoes (or tomato purée) if desired.

Chicken Filo Pie

JANE ASHER

Serves 6 Preparation time: 15-20 minutes Cooking time: 45 minutes

1 x 1.4kg (3lb) cooked chicken
175g (6oz) cream cheese (a low fat one, if you prefer)
salt and black pepper
a handful of chopped fresh tarragon
22.8cm (9") cake tin, loose bottomed
6 sheets filo pastry
150ml (1/4 pint) plain yoghurt
(again, low fat if you wish)
1 x 275g (10oz) sliced mushrooms (tinned)
olive oil (a light, non-virgin one is fine)

Filo is easy to handle, light to eat and can be used for sweet or savoury dishes. You can buy it frozen in 450g (1lb) packets which contain at least 24 sheets. Keep it in the freezer, transferring it to the fridge 12 hours before you want to use it. You can make all sorts of differently shaped parcels, from traditional triangles to mini crackers. Don't re-freeze any left over; return to the fridge, sealed in its original package. It will keep for a month. You can also find it fresh in many delicatessens and supermarkets.
NB Traditionally, filo pastry is brushed with melted butter, but I prefer using olive oil. It's far healthier and the result is less greasy. Make sure you use it between each layer. If this is not done, the under layers tend to remain uncooked.

Heat the oven to 350°F/180°C/gas mark 4. Remove the meat from the chicken carcass and shred it. Mix the cream cheese, yoghurt and tarragon and season with salt and black pepper. Combine the shredded chicken, drained mushrooms and cream cheese mixture and mix well.

Brush a loose-bottomed 22.8cm (9") diameter cake tin with butter. Brush five sheets of filo pastry with olive oil and line the cake tin so that the edges of the pastry overlap the top of the tin. Place the chicken mixture inside the tin on the pastry and fold over the edges of the pastry to enclose the chicken, brushing each layer lightly with oil. Oil the final sheet of pastry and cut into strips, then decorate the top of the pie with the strips. Cook in the pre-heated oven for 20 minutes. At the end of this time, take the pie from the oven, remove the sides of the cake tin, brush the edges of the pie with oil and return to the oven for 25 minutes or until the outside is golden brown. If the top starts to darken too much, cover with foil.

To serve, slide the pie off the base with a metal spatula and onto a warm serving dish.

Jane Asher

Chocolate Fudge Cake

SARAH BAILEY MBE

This recipe is a real pick me up and very naughty, but great to get the energy flowing again after a hard week in the pool. It's a special recipe my mum uses and it's magic!

For the cake:

6oz margarine
3 eggs
1oz custard powder
2 sandwich tins
6oz caster sugar
5oz self raising flour
1oz cocoa powder

Cream sugar and margarine together into a paste. Beat the eggs together and gradually add to the paste.
Sieve the flour, custard powder and cocoa powder into a separate bowl, then fold into the mixture.
Divide the mixture between the two tins.
Bake at 350°F/180°C/gas mark 4 for 20-25 minutes.
While the cake is baking, make the icing.

For the icing:

5oz margarine
1lb icing sugar
6 tablespoons hot milk
8 tablespoons cocoa
2 teaspoons vanilla essence

Melt margarine. Gradually add sifted cocoa powder, mix well. Slowly add sifted icing sugar, alternating it with adding hot milk. Add vanilla essence. Beat well to make smooth and shiny.
When the cakes are baked, turn out onto a cooling rack and allow to cool.
When cool, place a tray under the cooling rack and start to spread the icing on the bottom section of the cake, allow to drip onto the tray. Place the top section of the cake on the bottom and spread the remaining icing over the top. BE GENEROUS WITH THE ICING!
Decorate the top if you wish, my favourites include chocolate buttons, smarties and hundreds and thousands!
Serve with cream or ice cream - hot or cold.

Marmalade Ice Cream

THELMA BARLOW

3 large eggs
3oz caster sugar (flavoured with vanilla)
2 tablespoons frozen orange juice concentrate
1 dessertspoon brandy
3/4 pint of double cream
1 tablespoon cointreau
3 tablespoons dark marmalade

3 mixing bowls - yolks in one, whites in one and cream in the other.

2 oz of sugar in with yolks and beat till thick. Heat marmalade and brandy, cool and mix into yolks. Add juice and beat further.

Beat cream and 1oz of sugar till stiff and combine with yolk mix. Add cointreau.

Whip egg whites till peaks, fold lightly into mixture and freeze.

This is a favourite recipe of mine - really delicious!

Eliza's Strawberry Cake

MARTIN BASHIR

My favourite dessert is a lush summer pudding, which my five-year-old daughter, Eliza, calls 'strawberry cake'. It is so simple to make that even a television journalist would not struggle to complete the recipe.

You will need a mixture of fresh strawberries, raspberries and blackberries, plus eight ounces of caster sugar and a medium sliced loaf of white bread. Three pre-packaged boxes of strawberries, two of raspberries and two of blackberries is how I measure out the quantities!

Place all the fruit in a saucepan, with the sugar and two tablespoons of water. Cook gently for about twenty minutes, until the fruit is soft. Remove all the rind of every slice of the loaf.

Once cooked, strain the fruit and leave the juice to cool. Then dip the bread into the juice and line a glass bowl. Pour the fruit into the bread-lined bowl, add bread on top so that the fruit is entirely covered and then place overnight in a fridge.

To serve, turn the bowl upside down and a beautifully formed summer pudding should fall upon a plate. Garnish with extra thick, double cream, ignore your doctor's advice and enjoy! Eliza will be knocking at your door to share in this delightful dessert!

Custard Pie

JEREMY BEADLE

Serves 4 to eat or 1 good throw!

8oz short crust pastry
2 teaspoons sugar
vanilla essence
half pint milk
1 egg
grated nutmeg

Roll out the pastry to one third of an inch thick.

Line a round pie dish with the pastry and trim surplus with a sharp knife.

Warm the milk in a saucepan and add the sugar.

Beat the egg in a bowl and add the milk, gently stirring.

Add a few drops of vanilla essence and allow to cool slightly.

Pour the mixture into the pastry case.

Sprinkle with nutmeg.

Bake in a moderate oven at 350°C/180°C for about 30 minutes.

The pastry should be golden brown and the custard cooked and firm.

Strawberry Surprise

MARTIN BELL OBE

Serves 6

3 medium sized punnets of strawberries
caster sugar

Slice the strawberries from two of the punnets and arrange in a bowl.

Liquidise the third punnet into a puree and pour over the sliced strawberries.

Sprinkle lightly with caster sugar and serve with cream.

Pitta Pizzas

RAYMOND BLANC

Mozzarella and Tomato

This is only for the summer when your tomatoes are at their best.

1 large wholemeal pitta bread, cut in 2 across centre
1 mozzarella cheese, approx. 120g
1 small bunch of fresh basil
freshly ground black pepper
4 tablespoons chunky tomato sauce
4 large ripe plum tomatoes, cored
4 tablespoons olive oil

Preheat the oven to 200°C/400°F/gas mark 6.

Spread the tomato sauce over the top of the pitta. Slice the mozzarella and tomato to the same thickness. Layer them on top of the pitta bases. Tear the basil and sprinkle over, then douse with the olive oil and bake for 15 minutes. Give a good grind of black pepper, and serve.

Mascarpone, Spinach and Mushroom

1 wholemeal pitta bread
2 tablespoons olive oil
2 garlic cloves, peeled and crushed
100g spinach, leaves picked, washed and shredded
100g button mushrooms, washed and sliced
100g mascarpone cheese
1 small bunch of fresh parsley, leaves picked and chopped
salt and freshly ground black pepper
4 tablespoons chunky tomato sauce

Preheat the oven to 200°C/400°F/gas mark 6.

Warm the olive oil, add the garlic, spinach and mushrooms. Sauté over a high heat for 2 minutes without colouring, then decant into a colander and allow to cool. Once cooled, stir in the mascarpone and chopped parsley and season well.

Spread the tomato sauce across the pitta bread, then top with the spinach mixture, bake for 15 minutes and serve.

Chocolate Cake

CHERIE BOOTH QC

Suitable for freezing without the icing and decoration.

Makes 8 portions

- 100g (4oz) soft margarine
- 100g (4oz) cocoa powder
- 300g soft brown sugar
- 2 eggs
- 250ml milk
- 200g self-raising flower
- 1 tsp. baking powder

Fudge Topping

- 200g plain chocolate
- 175ml double cream
- 25g butter, diced

Pre-heat the oven to 180°C/gas 4. Cream together the margarine and sugar until light and fluffy. Beat the eggs and mix with the cocoa powder. Gradually add the egg and cocoa powder to the creamed margarine and sugar. Sift together the flour and baking powder and fold this into the first mixture, then gradually mix in the milk until well blended. Line and grease 2 x 8″ sandwich tins and spoon the mixture into each of the tins. Bake for about 30 minutes until risen and slightly firm to touch. Allow to cool down a little, then remove from the tins and place the cakes on a wire cooling rack.

To prepare the fudge topping: Heat the cream in a saucepan until boiling. Remove from the heat and stir in the chocolate, broken into pieces, until melted. Finally, beat in the butter. Allow to cool down a little before using this to sandwich the cakes together and also to cover the top and sides of the cake.

Risotto

JEREMY BOWEN

First, make some chicken stock. Put a chicken carcass, or the remains of a roast chicken in a pan, add an onion, some celery, a carrot, bay leaf and black pepper corns. Cook it for hours - skim off fat.

Fry an onion in olive oil and some butter. Add risotto rice (arborio or similar). Sauté with onion till grains all covered in oil. Add stock in small amounts, stirring all the time, until rice is 'al dente'.

Serve with freshly grated parmesan.

You can add celery, or similar, at start of cooking and then a bit more half way through if you like (season with salt and pepper).

Good cooking!
Jeremy Bowen

Garlic Chicken & Sherry

DAVID BROWN

Serves 4 - 6

3lb chicken thighs
2 tablespoons plain flour
3 garlics, about 30 cloves, peeled but left whole
3 bay leaves
salt and pepper to taste
4 fl oz extra virgin olive oil
7 fl oz dry sherry
dried thyme to sprinkle

Pat the chicken dry on a kitchen roll and season with salt and pepper. Dust lightly with the flour. Take a casserole dish or a heavy based frying pan with a lid and warm the olive oil.

Holly Oaks

Add the chicken and sauté over a medium heat until its golden brown. Remove the chicken with a slotted spoon and put to one side.

Add the garlic to the oil and sauté gently for about 2 minutes to soften. Pour in the sherry allowing it to bubble up and absorb the cooking juices.

Put the chicken back in the pan, add the bay leaves, cover and simmer over a moderate heat for about 35 minutes.

Sprinkle with the thyme and serve at once with new potatoes and green beans or any other vegetables.

Cullen Skink

KEN BRUCE

Typical fisherman's soup

Serves 4

1 large finnan haddock - use whole fish
half pint water
1 pint milk
$^1/_2$ lb mashed potato
fresh chopped parsley
half an onion
salt and pepper
1oz butter, cut into small pieces
4 tablespoons cream

Place the haddock in a saucepan with the onion, cover with the water. Bring to the boil and simmer for about 15 minutes. Remove the fish and separate the flesh from the skin and bones and set fish aside.

Return the skin and bones to the pan, season and cook for a further hour. Strain this fish stock, discarding the skin and bones, add the flaked fish.

Return to the heat, add the milk, butter and mashed potato. Bring to the boil and simmer for a few minutes. Adjust seasoning and stir a spoonful of cream into each bowl just before serving and add a garnish of chopped parsley.

Chocolate Crunch

EMMA BUNTON

4oz butter
2 teaspoons Golden Syrup
Galaxy chocolate, lots of it
cornflakes or rice krispies

Melt butter and chocolate on a low heat, add golden syrup. Add cornflakes or rice krispies, a handful at a time and stir until the chocolate mixture covers all the cornflakes or krispies. Place mixture into paper cake cases and put in the fridge.

Love ya loads
Emma xxx

Nut Roast fit for a King

BISHOP OF CHESTER

Serves 4 - 6

medium sized onion
8oz (225g) mixed nuts (peanuts, walnuts, cashews, hazelnuts)
half pint (300ml) vegetable stock or water
1 teaspoon mixed herbs
1oz (25g) butter/margarine
4oz (100g) wholemeal bread
2 teaspoons (10ml) yeast extract
(if using water)
salt and pepper to taste

Variations:
Include variety of chopped, sautéed vegetables
Add grated cheese between two layers of nut mixture

Chop onions and sauté in butter until transparent.

Grind nuts and bread together in food processor.

Heat stock or water and yeast extract.

Combine all ingredients well.

Turn into greased baking dish and level surface.

Sprinkle with a few breadcrumbs.

Bake in the oven at 180°C/350°F/gas mark 4 for
45 minutes until golden brown.

Garnish with fried onion rings.

+Peter Cestr

Cornflakes (breakfast dish)

JOHN CLEESE

Buy a packet of cornflakes;

Open the cardboard box;

Open the sort of plastic packet inside the box;

Pour the contents (sort of yellowy-brownish bits of things) on to a plate;

Buy a bottle of milk;

Take the top off the thin end of the bottle;

Invert the bottle gently over the cornflakes making sure that the milk does not go over the edge of the plate.

It's very simple to make and absolutely delicious.

An alternative is to use coca-cola instead of milk.

Add basil as required!

Louise's Bread & Butter Pudding

MAX CLIFFORD

This is a favourite recipe of mine as made by my daughter, Louise - made with croissants and chocolate chips!

2 pint oval enamel dish (greased with butter)
11 fl oz milk
3 large eggs
2oz milk chocolate chips
zest of a lemon (optional)
4-5 medium croissants
3 fl oz double cream
3oz caster sugar
2oz sultanas
some brown sugar (for sprinkling on the top)

Slice the croissants into thin slices (approx 1/2"). Line the surface of the bowl with the croissant slices, use end pieces to fill any gaps. Sprinkle half of the sultanas and some of the chocolate chips. Repeat the process, using the remaining sultanas and some more of the chocolate chips. Place another layer of croissants and the last of the chocolate chips.

Take a jug and mix the milk, cream and sugar and add the pre-whisked eggs. Stir to combine all the ingredients. Add lemon zest if using and pour over the croissants. Sprinkle with the brown sugar and cook in 180°C pre-heated oven for 35-40 minutes or until pudding has absorbed all the liquid.

Pasta Primavera

JOAN COLLINS

Serves 4

Once spurned by dieters, there has been a re-think on pasta and it is now recognised as an excellent source of complex carbohydrates and one of the perfect energy foods. Choose wholewheat pasta as it contains fibre and serve it with a light tomato and herb sauce, but do not be tempted into topping it with a rich or a cream sauce high in calories. This is one of my favourite recipes for pasta.

500g penne
2 medium sized courgettes
8 large mushrooms
2 cloves garlic
1 broccoli head
2 medium sized onions
2 large tomatoes
grated parmesan cheese (optional)

Cook the pasta in boiling water for 12 minutes (until *al dente*). Drain and refresh with boiling water (removing excess starch). Break the broccoli head into florets and cook in the steamer or colander over boiling water. Steam for seven minutes approximately (so that the broccoli is cooked, but still crunch).
Chop the onions coarsely and sauté in a little butter until soft. (If you have a microwave, no butter is needed. Put the onions in a bowl with about 1/2" water on the bottom. Cover with cling film and cook at a high temperature for 2 1/2 minutes. When cooked, drain and add to the broccoli.)
Wash the courgettes and cut into 2" strips. Cook in the steamer for about 5 minutes or boil in water until cooked but not too soft. Clean the mushrooms with a little salt and kitchen paper (or you can peel them). Place under a hot grill for a few minutes. Drain on kitchen paper. When cooked, cut into large chunks.
Concasse the tomatoes by placing them in boiling water for 10 seconds, then transferring them immediately to cold water. This allows you to remove the skin. Quarter and cut each quarter in half again. Remove seeds.
Crush the garlic and add to the vegetables. Season with salt and pepper. Add the vegetables (except the broccoli) to the pasta and reheat gently in a saucepan.
Place the broccoli back in the steamer for a minute to reheat and then carefully add to the hot pasta and vegetables. This prevents the broccoli from breaking up.
Add a little grated parmesan for more flavour, but this is not essential. Serve warm - not too hot.

It's scrumptious and another healthy dish that children will savour.

Phil's Tea

PHIL COLLINS

I drink this tea before and during my concerts and when I'm recording, as I find it very good for my throat.

Take a large pinch of loose peppermint tea, a large pinch of comfrey tea and a small pinch of gold seal tea. Place all in a teapot and add boiling water. Meanwhile, in a thermos flask, squeeze the juice of half a lemon and add approximately two teaspoons of honey (depending on your taste). Add liberal pinch of cayenne pepper (I use a lot!). When the tea is brewed - allowing normal time - pour into flask, shake well and drink.

Devilled Chicken

ROSEMARY CONLEY

Serves 4 Per serving (excluding rice and salad): 177kcal/8.1g fat

4 skinless chicken breasts
2 tablespoons dijon mustard
1 tablespoon soy sauce
2 teaspoons freshly chopped ginger
salt and freshly ground black pepper
300ml (half pint) tomato juice
1 red chilli, seeded and finely chopped
2 teaspoons paprika
2 tablespoons chopped fresh parsley

Although this dish is quite mild, you can make it hotter by adding more chilli if desired.

Place the chicken breasts in an ovenproof dish or on a baking sheet. Season well on both sides.

Combine the remaining ingredients in a bowl and spoon over the chicken breasts. Place in a preheated oven at 190°C/375°F/gas mark 5 and cook for 25-30 minutes until the juices run clear.

Serve with boiled rice mixed with peas and a side salad.

Photograph: Alan Olley

Tuna Bake

SHARRON DAVIES

Easy and quick, takes about 10 minutes to prepare and 30 minutes to cook.

large tin of tuna - dolphin friendly only
small tin of sweetcorn
butter, milk, salt and pepper to taste
small tomato
1 onion
packet of smash instant potato
4oz grated cheese

Put oven on medium heat.

Prepare instant potato to taste.

Fry onions, add tuna when nearly done and salt and pepper to taste.

Mix in sweetcorn, put in ovenproof dish. Add a layer of grated cheese (about half).

Add thick layer of potato, decorate with sliced tomato, sprinkle with remainder of cheese.

Bake in oven for 20 to 30 minutes until hot.

Serve with salad and fresh bread - *yummm!*

Chocolate Surprise Pudding

BOBBY DAZZLER

150g (5oz) self raising flour
200g (7oz) golden caster sugar
175ml (6fl oz) full cream milk
50g (2oz) unsalted butter, melted
fresh mint, to decorate
25g (1oz) cocoa powder
75g (3oz) mint-flavoured chocolate, chopped
2 teaspoons vanilla essence
1 medium egg

Sauce:
175g (6oz) dark muscovado sugar
125g (4oz) cocoa powder
600ml (1 pint) very hot water

Pre-heat the oven to 180°C/350°F/gas mark 4.

10 minutes before baking, lightly oil a 2½ pint ovenproof dish. Sift the flour and cocoa powder into a large bowl and stir in the caster sugar and chopped mint-flavoured chocolate and make a well in the centre.

Whisk the milk, vanilla essence and the melted butter together, then beat in the egg. Pour into the well and gradually mix together, drawing the dry ingredients in from the side of the bowl. Beat until mixed thoroughly. Spoon into the prepared dish.

To make the sauce, blend the dark muscovado sugar and the cocoa powder together and spoon over the top of the pudding. Carefully pour the hot water over the top of the pudding, but do not mix.

Bake in the pre-heated oven for 35-40 minutes or until firm to the touch and the mixture has formed a sauce underneath. Decorate with mint and serve immediately.

Rillette of Duck with Homemade Brioche

HAMISH DEAS

A very versatile dish, which is great for any occasion be it snacking, picnic or a dinner party to impress. It is a dish best made the day before, but keeps well for about a week in the fridge.

Rillette of Duck

2 duck legs
2 sticks of celery
sprig of thyme
water
2 teaspoons green peppercorns
2 carrots, peeled
1 small onion
1 bay leaf
6oz white wine (1 glass)

Trim fat and skin from the duck legs and mince down coarsely. Mince carrots, onion and celery.

Place minced fat, vegetables, white wine and herbs in a pan and cook until all the liquid has gone. Put the two duck legs and green peppercorns in and cover with water. Cook slowly until the meat is stringy (approx. 1½ hours).

Remove from heat and pick out the bones and mash remaining mixture with a fork. Put mixture into ramekins and chill overnight. Turn out and serve with brioche.

Brioche

1lb strong flour
teaspoon of sugar
4 eggs
½ pint warmed milk
1oz fresh yeast
pinch of salt
3oz melted butter

Put flour, eggs, salt and butter into a bowl and mix. Cream yeast with sugar and mix into flour. Add warm milk gradually to flour mixture, mixing until a firm dough is achieved. Knead this dough for 5 minutes. Leave in a warm place to prove until it is double its size. Knock back and knead for a further 5 minutes. Roll into balls, leave to prove and bake at 180° for 5-8 minutes.

HAMISH DEAS

Head Chef, Etrop Grange

Bread & Butter Pudding

Dame JUDI DENCH

Half pint of milk (275ml)
Grated rind of half a small lemon
3 eggs
half oz candied lemon or orange peel (10g) finely chopped
freshly grated nutmeg
One eighth pint double cream (70ml)
2oz caster sugar (50g)
Pannetone cake
2oz currants (50g)

Pre-heat oven to gas 4/350°F/180°C.

Butter a 2 pint (1 litre) oblong enamel baking dish.

Slice the Pannetone and butter it. Put one layer on the base of the dish, sprinkle with the candied peel and half the currants. Put another layer of Pannetone in the dish and sprinkle with the rest of the currants.

Put the milk and cream together in a measuring jug, stir in the lemon peel and sugar. Whisk the eggs in a small basin and add to the milk mixture. Pour the whole lot over the Pannetone and sprinkle with freshly grated nutmeg.

Bake in the oven for 30-40 minutes. Serve warm.

This is delicious and provides the perfect solution for what to do with those dry Italian cakes you get given at Christmas!

Judi Dench

Malva Pudding

DUKE OF DEVONSHIRE

Pudding

1 cup sugar
1 tablespoon apricot jam
1 teaspoon bicarbonate of soda
1 tablespoon butter
1 cup milk
1 egg
1 cup flour
generous pinch of salt
1 teaspoon vinegar

Beat the egg and sugar well in a mixer. Add the jam.

Sift flour, bicarbonate of soda and salt.

Melt the butter and add the vinegar.

Add liquids to egg mixture alternately with the flour.

Beat well and bake in a covered dish at 350°F for three quarters of an hour.

Sauce

half cup cream
1 cup sugar
half cup butter
half cup milk
half cup hot water

Melt together the ingredients for the sauce and pour over the pudding as it comes out of the oven.

Dried Fruit Compote

BARBARA DICKSON

dried prunes	apricots
apples	pears
figs	stick of cinnamon
8 cloves	greek yoghurt

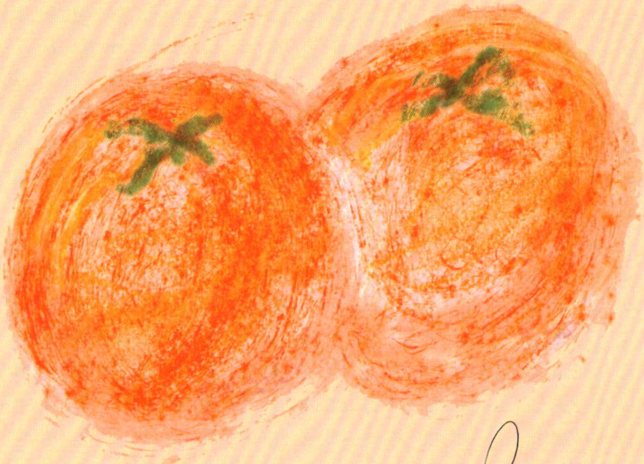

Take a handful of each of dried prunes, apricots, apples, pears and figs. Add enough water to cover in a saucepan.

Cook until tender with a stick of cinnamon and about 8 cloves. (You can also use tea to cook - strained of course!)

When cooked, remove from heat and when cold serve with a HUGE dollop of Greek yoghurt.

Delicious.

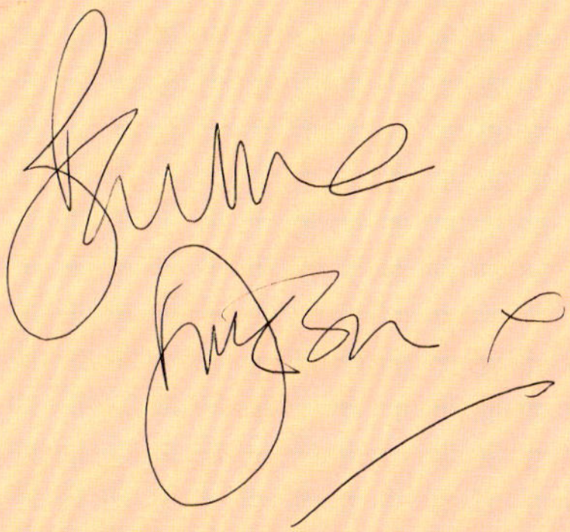

Hock with Cider & Raisins

CHARLIE DIMMOCK

Serves 6 **Preparation time: 20 minutes** **Cooking time: 2 1/2 hours**

Bacon, cooked with dried peas or beans, is one of the oldest known English dishes, dating back to the 14th century. The following is a 20th century version of the medieval recipe.

2-2 1/2 lb back or shoulder of gammon
1 small onion
2 tablespoons chopped celery
1 1/2 oz butter
2 teaspoons demerara sugar
1/4 pint gammon stock
1/2 lb split peas, lentils or chick peas
1 1/2 oz plain flour
2oz stoneless raisins
1/2 pint dry cider
2 tablespoons chopped parsley

Wash the hock and place it in a large bowl, together with the peas or lentils. Cover with cold water and leave to soak for 8 hours or overnight. Drain the meat and peas, put them in a large heavy-based pan and cover with fresh cold water. Bring to the boil, then lower the heat and cover the pan with a lid. Simmer for 1 1/2 hours or until the hock is tender.
Lift the meat from the pan and set it aside to cool slightly. Leave the peas to cook for a further 30-40 minutes or until quite tender. Skin the hock carefully while still warm, and cut the meat into 1" cubes, discarding the fat.
Peel and finely chop the onion and prepare the celery. Melt the butter in a heavy-based pan over moderate heat, fry the onion and celery for a few minutes until soft. Remove the pan from the heat and stir in the flour until it has absorbed all the butter. Gradually stir in the cider to make a smooth sauce. Return the pan to the heat and bring the sauce to simmering point, stirring continuously. Mix in the raisins, and add sufficient gammon stock to make a creamy sauce. Blend in the sugar and continue cooking and stirring over a low heat for a further 10 minutes.
Add the cubed hock to the cider sauce, heating it through thoroughly and stirring occasionally. Drain the peas or lentils thoroughly and toss them in a little butter and parsley. Spoon the meat and sauce into the centre of a warmed serving dish and surround with a border of the peas.
Alternatively, make the peas into chick patties.

Seared Tuna Steak

STEVEN DOHERTY

Served with Egg Noodles & a Soy, Ginger and Spring Onion Dressing

Serves 4 Preparation time: 10-15 minutes Cooking time: 5 minutes

A truly wonderful and very easy dish - inspired by my many visits to Manchester's China Town.

Steven Doherty

4 pre-cut tuna steaks 4½oz (125g) each
10 fl oz (300ml) sunflower oil
6 spring onions, finely sliced

¼ teaspoon of minced garlic
salt and freshly ground pepper
1 lime

1 pack egg noodles
soy sauce
1 tablespoon freshly grated ginger
1 tablespoon sesame oil
plain flour

Dressing Whisk together 7 fl oz (200ml) of sunflower oil with 3½ fl oz (100ml) of soy sauce. Add the ginger, garlic, sesame oil, sliced spring onions, a couple of twists of ground pepper and the dressing is now ready.

Noodles Cook the noodles in boiling, salted water as per packet instructions, place under running cold water then drain in a colander and drizzle with a little oil to stop them from sticking. Pre-heat a small roasting dish and gently re-heat the noodles 'dry' in a low oven.

Tuna Flour and season the tuna, pour 3 fl oz (75ml) of sunflower oil into the frying pan and heat the oil until nearly smoking. Add the tuna immediately and cook for 60 seconds each side. Remove the fish from the pan and place onto kitchen paper.

To serve Arrange the noodles on the plate, place the fish on top and spoon over the dressing. Decorate with some fresh coriander and a wedge of lime.

NB The dressing must be kept at kitchen temperature and should be whisked before serving to blend the soy and oil together.

Classic Sour Cream Cheesecake

HUW EDWARDS

This is an excellent English recipe for plain cheesecake which is easy to make and always popular with the children! The quality of the vanilla extract can make all the difference, so spend a little more on this if you can. Using low fat cream cheese is also perfectly good - and a little less damaging . . .

16 small shortbread biscuits
24oz softened cream cheese
4 eggs
1 tablespoon good quality vanilla extract
2 large knobs margarine or butter, melted
14oz sweetened condensed milk
8oz sour cream

Pre-heat the oven to 350°F.

Break up the biscuits and blend them with the butter or margarine. Press the mixture into the bottom of a 9" springform tin. In a large mixer bowl beat the cheese until quite fluffy. Gradually beat in the sweetened condensed milk until smooth. Then beat in the eggs, followed by the sour cream and vanilla extract. Pour into the prepared tin.

Bake for around 50 minutes or until lightly browned around the edge (the centre will be slightly soft). Cool and then chill. It can be left plain or garnished with lemon slices.

Huw Edwards

Veg Pie

DAVID ESSEX

1 portion ready-made short crust pastry or your own favourite pie crust recipe

1 medium courgette, sliced
2oz hazelnuts
1 clove garlic, crushed
1 small aubergine, diced into triangles
1 small jar of traditional pasta sauce

1 medium onion, diced
parmesan cheese
1 yellow pepper, sliced
1 single portion size of broccoli (boiled for 10 minutes and drained)

Put a tablespoon of sunflower oil into a frying pan, add garlic and onion and cook until the onions are transparent and soft, stirring continuously so the garlic doesn't burn.

Add courgette, pepper and aubergine, cook until the aubergine slices darken and soften, add the broccoli and stir for a few more minutes.
Now stir in three quarters of the pasta sauce, spoon the vegetables into a medium size oven dish, roll out the pastry, spread the remainder of the pasta sauce evenly over the vegetable mixture, sprinkle with parmesan cheese and a small handful of hazelnuts to taste.

Cover with the pastry, seal the edges with a rolling pin.

Bake in a moderately hot oven for 25-30 minutes or until the pastry is cooked.

Grilled Sea Bass with Fettucine & Ratatouille Sauce

Sir ALEX FERGUSON CBE

Serves 4

450g (1lb) pasta dough
50g (2oz) unsalted butter
Salt and fresh ground black pepper
4 sea bass fillets (about 175-225g [6-8oz] each)
25ml (1fl oz) olive oil

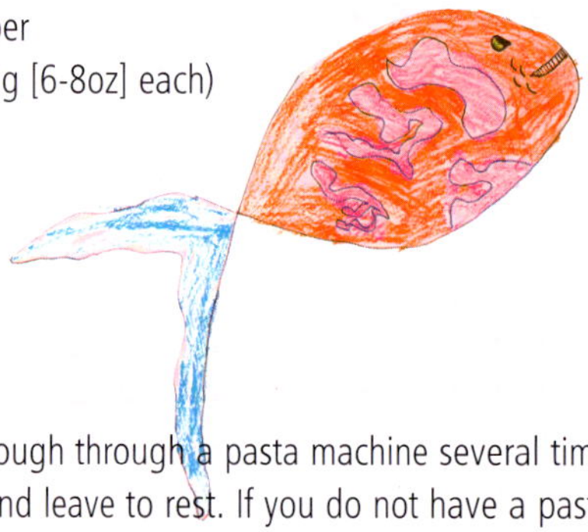

For the Ratatouille Sauce
1 red pepper, seeded
1 green pepper, seeded
2 shallots
Half an aubergine
25g (1oz) unsalted butter
25g (1fl oz) olive oil
300ml (10fl oz) red pepper coulis
1 courgette

To make the fettucine: Roll the dough through a pasta machine several times until it becomes about 1mm thick (1/16"), then pass through the noodle cutter and leave to rest. If you do not have a pasta machine, it can be divided, rolled several times until very thin, then cut by hand into ribbons; a pizza wheel is the easiest way to cut the pasta.

Pre-heat the grill to medium, add butter and season a flameproof baking tray.

To make the ratatouille: Dice the vegetables. Melt the butter with the olive oil in a large pan. Add the diced vegetables and cook for about 3-4 minutes until just softened. In another pan, warm the red pepper coulis then add the vegetables. Season with salt and pepper.

Lay the sea bass fillets on the prepared tray, skin side up and cook under the medium grill for about 8 minutes.

While the fish is cooking, boil a large pan of water with the olive oil and a pinch of salt. When boiling, drop in the pasta and move it around with a fork. If it is fresh, it will only take a few minutes to cook. For dried pasta, just follow the instructions on the packet. Drain through a colander, season with salt and pepper and toss with the remaining butter to loosen.

Warm the ratatouille sauce and spoon it on hot plates. Sit the fettucine in the middle and lay the grilled sea bass on the top.

I hope that you enjoy this dish as much as I do!

Alex. Ferguson

Parkin

JAMES GALWAY

4oz margarine
3oz light brown sugar
4oz medium oatmeal
pinch of bicarbonate of soda
1 level teaspoon of mixed spice
1/4 pint of milk
8oz treacle
4oz self raising flour
1 tablespoon marmalade
1 level teaspoon ground ginger
1 egg

Grease and line an 8" square tin.

Put margarine, marmalade, treacle and sugar in a pan and warm.

Add milk and leave to cool.

Add all dry ingredients.

Add beaten egg and mix well.

Bake for 50-60 minutes at 180°C/gas mark 4.

Beef Wellington

DAVID GOWER

Serves 6-8

3lb beef fillet
1/2 lb finely chopped mushrooms
beaten egg to glaze
salt and pepper
1/4 lb paté
1lb puff pastry (or shortcrust)
1 tablespoon oil

Pre-heat oven to 230°C/425°F.

Rub beef with salt, pepper and oil. Roast on a rack for 40 minutes. Remove and leave to cool.

When cool, cover the top and sides with the paté and chopped mushrooms.

Roll out the pastry to quarter inch thickness - large enough to envelope the meat. Put the fillet top side down on the pastry, and enclosed into a parcel sealing the ends. Turn meat seam side down and decorate with spare pastry if you can be be bothered! Glaze with the beaten egg.

Bake for a further 40 minutes or so, till the pastry is golden brown and puffed up.

Tastes even better if served with a red wine sauce.

Steak & Kidney Pud

RUSSELL GRANT

Serves 4

Suet Crust:
8oz (225g) plain flour
4oz (100g) shredded suet
salt
cold water

Filling:
1lb (450g) chuck steak, cubed
4oz (100g) ox kidney, cut up
seasoned flour
dripping (beef for preference) for frying
2 onions

Gravy:
2 beef cubes
1 teaspoon each of
worcestershire sauce & marmite
Make up to a pint (600ml)
with hot water

To make the suet pastry, mix flour, suet and little salt and add enough cold water to make a dough. Allow to rest before rolling out.

Roll the steak and kidney in seasoned flour and gently fry in beef dripping to seal in flavour. Fry the onions for about a minute.

Roll out pastry and line a 2 pint (1 litre) size basin, leaving enough pastry to make a lid.

Put in the steak, kidney and onions and pour in gravy, but not enough to fill the basin. Put on the pastry lid and seal the edges well. Cover with greaseproof paper and kitchen foil and steam for 4 to 5 hours.

Serve with mashed spuds and cabbage.

Tip: When eating alone I make a smaller pudding by making up half the quantities, omits the kidney and uses a good quality tin of chuck steak. This reduces cooking time to about an hour because the tinned steak is already cooked. I also give the pastry a bit of 'interest' by adding some cut up pieces of fried bacon.

For a richer gravy, use half water and half Guinness.

Spicy Prawn Casserole

TANNI GREY-THOMPSON OBE

200g prawns (or white fish) per person
1 tablespoon olive oil
2-3 cloves garlic
1 tin of tomatoes
1 onion
1-2 red or green chillis (or 2 teaspoons chilli sauce/paste)
4oz mushrooms (sliced)
2oz long grain rice per person
cardamom pods
feta or mozzarella cheese
fresh basil

Cook for 20 minutes hob or oven 180°C

Finely chop onion, chilli and garlic and fry in olive oil until softened. Add all other ingredients, adding the fish last. Either gently simmer on hob or oven cook for 15 minutes, adding the cheese for the last five minutes of cooking time when the sauce should have thickened.

Meanwhile, cook the rice according to instructions, rinse the rice with boiling water and strain well adding the cardamom pods. Serve the fish and sauce on a bed of rice and garnish with the fresh basil.

Best wishes

Tanni

Griddled Salmon with Garlic & Basil White Beans

LOYD GROSSMAN

Serves 4

Fish and beans complement each other very well in a meal. This dish uses a can of cannellini beans in a quick pan-fry sauce. All it needs is some crusty white bread to mop up the delicious juices.

4 fillets salmon, about 125g each
1 lemon, cut into wedges
1 fat clove garlic, crushed
420g can cannellini white beans, drained
about 6 large leaves fresh basil, torn in strips
2-3 tablespoons extra virgin olive oil
1 small onion, thinly sliced
2 tomatoes, skinned and chopped roughly
small knob of butter or 1 tablespoon creme fraiche
sea salt and freshly ground black pepper

Brush the salmon fillets with half the oil, season lightly and cook either in a pre-heated iron ridged griddle for about 3-5 minutes each side or under a pre-heated grill. The fish is cooked when it feels firm. Remove and squeeze over a little lemon juice. Set aside.

Sauté the onion, garlic and chopped tomato in the remaining oil for about 5 minutes until softened then stir in the beans. Heat until bubbling and cook for a couple of minutes, then beat in the butter or creme fraiche, some seasoning and the basil. Remove from the heat and spoon alongside the salmon to serve.

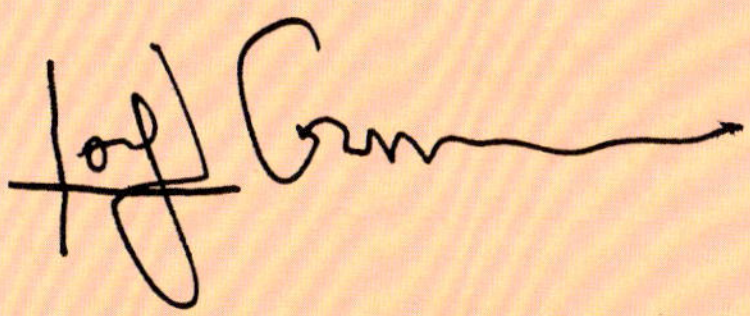

Welsh Cakes

FFION HAGUE

8oz self raising flour
4oz granulated sugar
half teaspoon of cinnamon
a pinch of salt
4oz butter
2oz sultanas or currants
1 beaten egg

Sieve the flour, cinnamon and salt into a large bowl and add the butter. Rub together until the mixture resembles fine breadcrumbs. Add the sugar and mix well.

Wet the mixture with the beaten egg and knead it into a dough. Add the dried fruit and knead the dough again until the fruit is evenly distributed.

Roll out the dough on a floured surface and cut with a pastry cutter into small cakes. Cook the cakes on both sides over a low heat on a griddle or ungreased frying pan until they are golden brown.
Delicious served warm or cold.

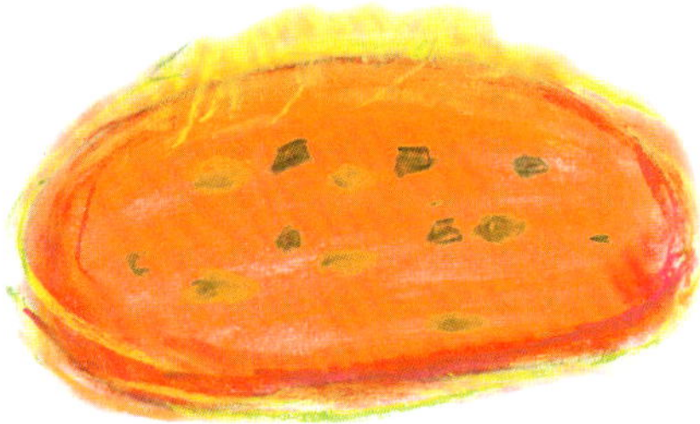

Yours, Ffion Hague

Broth of Asparagus, Wild Mushroom & New Potatoes

PAUL HEATHCOTE

Serves 2

150ml chicken stock (or water)
6 spears of asparagus
50g butter
truffle oil (optional)
salt, pepper and lemon juice
6 cooked new potatoes
50g wild mushrooms
sprig of parsley
dash of cream

Cook and refresh asparagus and parsley.

Warm the stock, add mushrooms and new potatoes.

Add a dash of cream and whisk in butter.

Re-heat asparagus in broth, add parsley, season and adjust with lemon juice.

Black Eyed Beans with Cinnamon & Tomatoes

MARGARET HICKIE
Senior Nurse, Francis House

8oz black eyed beans
12oz of firm tomatoes (or a tin)
2 medium onions, thinly sliced
2 teaspoons ground cinnamon
2 teaspoons tomato purée
1 pint water
4 teaspoons olive oil
1 large clove garlic, finely chopped
1/2 pint stock

Soak the beans overnight then simmer for 30 minutes. Drain if necessary.

Scald, skin and de-seed tomatoes. Cut them into strips. Heat the oil in a saucepan on a low heat. Stir in the onions and garlic and cook until the onions are soft. Stir in the beans and cinnamon, cover them and cook them gently for 2 minutes. Pour in the stock and bring it to the boil. Mix in the tomato purée, cover and simmer for 20 minutes so that the beans pick up a 'cinnamony' flavour. Mix in the tomatoes just before serving, so they heat through but stay firm.

Serve with rice, pasta, potato or even toast!

Pumpkin Soup

THORA HIRD

Serves 6

I don't cook much myself, since turning 90 on my last birthday, but I would like to share the following recipe with you. My daughter is a wonderful cook and this soup is excellent. She has a large garden and therefore grows her own pumpkins, so I'll let her tell you the recipe in her own words.

Ideal for a Hallowe'en party or to be served at Harvest Festival time. This has been a family favourite for years! This is a beautiful autumnal dish, golden in colour and warm in flavour. Even better if made a day in advance and reheated! If you have the time, hollow out an extra pumpkin and use it as a soup tureen with its own lid. It makes a splendid centrepiece!

1/2 cup butter
1 onion, finely chopped
1 teaspoon ground cumin
1/2lb (8oz) celery root, cut into chunks
salt and pepper
3 tablespoons chopped parsley (to garnish)
1 tablespoon sunflower oil
1 teaspoon ground coriander
1/2lb (8oz) pumpkin cut into chunks
3 3/4 cups of hot chicken stock
1/2lb (8oz) tomatoes, skinned and chopped (or tinned)

Heat half the butter and all the oil in a saucepan and cook the onion until transparent. Add the spices and cook for 2-3 minutes, stirring. Add the pumpkin and celery root and cook gently for 4-5 minutes, stirring. Add the stock, bring to boil and simmer for 25 minutes, half covered, till the celery root is soft. Add salt and pepper to taste.

Meanwhile, melt remaining butter in small frying pan and cook tomatoes 3-4 minutes, then add them to the soup. Allow the soup to cool slightly, then puree it briefly in a food processor, stopping before it is totally smooth. Reheat and pour into a warmed tureen or pumpkin shell warmed through in the oven. Serve sprinkled with parsley.

Variation For vegetarians, substitute vegetable stock for chicken stock.

PRIVATE EYE

Ian Hislop (Domestic God) chooses his favourite recipe.

Frostie's

1. Pour Frostie's into bowl.
2. Add Milk (To taste)
3. Serve cold.
4. er...
5. That's it.

Ian Hislop.

Champ

EAMONN HOLMES

Serves 4

This is a delicious Irish speciality which is simple and quick to cook. It should be served with plenty of melted butter drizzling down - but the health conscious can reduce this.

900g (2lb) floury potatoes
25g (1oz) butter
salt and freshly ground black pepper
spring onions
4 tablespoons milk
knobs of butter to serve

In separate pans, boil the potatoes and onions in lightly salted water until tender (the onions will cook for a much shorter time than the potatoes). Drain both and mash the potatoes in a bowl with the butter and the milk. Add the onions to the potatoes and mix in with some seasoning.

Heap into a bowl and make a hollow in the centre of the mash. Add extra knobs of butter and serve immediately.

Eamonn x

Single Man's Pasta Sauce

JOHN HUMPHRYS

I hope this recipe is suitable. I fear I am not the world's greatest cook!

Slice red and green peppers and red onions and sprinkle liberally with black pepper and good olive oil;

Put in a covered dish and microwave for a few minutes;

Add a can of chopped tomatoes and some thickening;

Return to microwave for another few minutes;

Cover a plate of fresh pasta with the resulting mix.

It not only tastes good; it's very healthy and - most important for a single man - there's only one dish to wash up afterwards!

Gloria's Mushroom Chicken

GLORIA HUNNIFORD

Serves 4

50g (2oz) butter
4 skinless chicken breasts
2 onions, sliced
2 garlic cloves, crushed
225g (8oz) mushrooms
300ml (10 fl oz) milk
295g (10oz) can condensed mushroom soup
15ml (1 tablespoon) tomato purée
dash of Tabasco sauce
dash of sherry (optional)
salt and pepper

Preheat the oven to 180°C/350°F/gas 4.

Melt the butter in a pan and brown the chicken breasts all over. Remove from the pan with a slotted spoon and arrange in an ovenproof dish. Fry the onions and garlic in the fat remaining in the pan until the onions are translucent.

Add the mushrooms and cook for 2-3 minutes. Add the milk and simmer gently for 3 minutes, then add the soup, tomato purée, Tabasco sauce and sherry, if using. Season with salt and pepper.

Pour the sauce over the chicken, cover the dish and cook for about 1 hour - until the chicken is cooked and tender.

Variation:
This sauce is equally as good served with fish or prawns.

Champ

JEREMY IRONS

Serves 4

$1\frac{1}{2}$ lb freshly cooked mashed potato
10 spring onions (or 2 leeks) cooked in $\frac{1}{2}$ cup of milk
4 tablespoons melted butter
salt and pepper

Cook the chopped spring onions, green part as well as white, in the milk. Drain and keep the milk. Mash the potatoes, season to taste and add the spring onions. Beat well together and add enough hot milk to make the dish creamy and smooth.

Place the mixture in a deep, warmed dish, making a well in the centre and pour the hot, melted butter into well. The dry potato should be dipped in the pool of butter when serving.

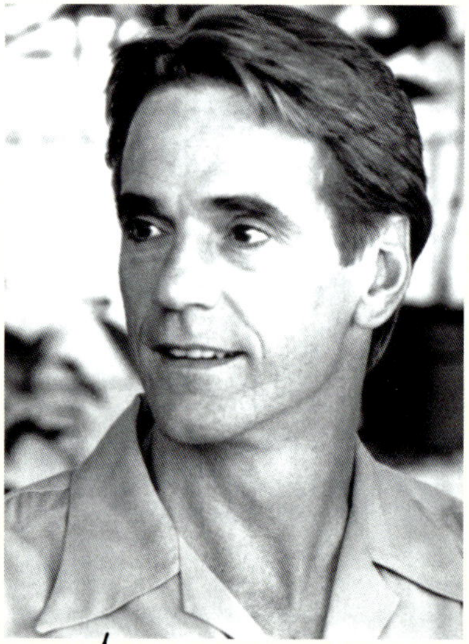

Champ can also be made with chopped parsley, chives, young nettle tops or young green peas. In the latter case, the peas are kept whole and added last. For a supper dish, scrambled eggs are often served in the centre and sprinkled with chopped parsley.

My great grandmother was Irish and she has passed on to me a great love of the potato. This dish will not cost much to make in time or trouble - yet on a winter's night it will kindle the coldest heart.

Savoury Cheese & Onion Flan

DEAN JENKINS

Dean Jenkins is one of the unsung heroes of the Hospice, working at the hub of all that goes on in the home as chief chef. Everything radiates out, including some amazing aromas, to all corners and to all people. The recipe he has chosen – Dean's Dish of the Day - is popular with the children, the parents and the staff of the Francis House family.

Shortcrust pastry

8oz plain flour
2oz butter
2-3 tablespoons cold water
2oz soft margarine
pinch of salt

Sieve the flour and the salt. Rub in the margarine and the butter to make a sandy texture.
Make a well in the centre, add sufficient water to make a fairly firm pastry.
Handle as little as possible and try to keep hands and equipment cold.
Lightly grease a large size flan dish. Line the dish with the pastry. Prick the bottom of the pastry with a fork.
Cook in a hot oven (230-250°C) for 4-8 minutes or until pastry is lightly set.

Remove from the oven and press the pastry down if it has tended to rise.

Savoury filling

3 eggs
2oz chopped onions
2oz single cream
4oz cheddar cheese - grated
8oz milk
pinch of salt and pepper

Mix the eggs, milk, cream and salt and pepper together. Put the cheese and onion in the cooked flan dish.
Strain the egg mixture over the cheese and onion, mix and cover with tin foil.
Return to the oven and bake for 30 minutes at 230°C, remove the tin foil and gently let the flan brown nicely.

Can be served hot or cold.

Roulades of Lemon Sole

COLIN JONES

Served with a Saffron Fish Cream Sauce and New Potatoes

Per person

1 8oz fillet of lemon sole (skinned)
2fl oz white wine
1 large carrot
2 florets of cauliflower
2 baby turnips
1 small swede
3 cocktail sticks
3 fl oz double cream

4oz baby spinach (picked and washed)
2fl oz fish stock (fresh or cubes)
2 florets of broccoli
2 baby carrots
3 new potatoes
2 grams saffron
1 fl oz olive oil
juice of 1 lemon

Lay fish on board, skin side up. Place spinach at tail end in a roll then carefully roll together. When rolled, pin with 3 cocktail sticks from one end to the other. Place on a foiled tray with olive oil.

Prepare fish sauce. Reduce white wine and fish stock with a few strands of saffron until half amount, then whisk in double cream. Add salt and pepper to taste and a squeeze of lemon juice.

Peel potatoes, cut into barrel shapes and place in a pan of seasoned water with remaining saffron and cook until *al dente*.

Peel vegetables and cut into desired shapes (ie. squares, florets and triangles for effect) then blanche and cool.

Bake sole in oven for 8-10 minutes on 250°C. Heat saffron sauce and place potatoes and vegetables into boiling water. When sole is ready, put in centre of plate and strain vegetables and potatoes from water and coat in olive oil and seasoning. Place saffron potatoes in each gap of the sole and arrange vegetables around the edge of the plate. Carefully pour the saffron sauce around the fish and finish with a drizzle of herb oil around the vegetables.

Colin Jones

Head Chef, Old Vicarage

Eezy Peezy Pizza

LORRAINE KELLY

Serves 4

Making pizza has never been easier! Here's how to transform ready-made pizza bases into something spectacular.

1 x 10oz (290g) packet pizza dough mix or 4 x 3oz (75g) ready made pizza bases

Sauce Topping:
14oz (400g) tin chopped tomatoes
1 tablespoon tomato purée
1 onion, finely chopped
1 teaspoon chilli powder
OR
1 jar Ragu or ready made pasta tomato sauce
3 large red peppers cut into thick strips
8oz (225g) large flat mushrooms,sliced
1 and a half tablespoons dried basil
3oz (75g) chopped almonds or any nuts
2oz (50g) parmesan
2oz (50g) grated cheddar cheese
12 pitted olives (optional)
3 tablespoons olive oil
salt and pepper

Preheat the oven to 200°C/400°F/gas mark 6. Make up the pizza bases according to the instructions on the packet and place on a greased baking tray.

Simmer the tomatoes, tomato puree, onion and chilli powder together in a saucepan for 8-10 minutes until thick and reduced. Spread tomato mixture over the pizza base (or, if using ready-made tomato sauce, spread sauce from jar over pizza base). Scatter over the peppers and mushrooms and season well with salt and pepper. Sprinkle over the dried basil, the almonds (or nuts) and the parmesan. Scatter over the cheese and olives. Drizzle over 3 tablespoons of olive oil and bake for 15-20 minutes or until bubbling hot and golden brown.

Serve at once.

Seg's Yorkshire Pudding

MATTHEW KELLY

4oz plain flour
3 eggs
pinch of salt
1/2 pint warm milky water
(2 tablespoons milk topped up with warm water)

Put flour and salt into a mixing bowl. Add the three eggs and beat vigorously. Gradually add the warm milk and water to the mixture until it becomes a thin cream.

Leave to stand for about half an hour.

Put a roasting tin in the oven with enough lard or oil to cover the bottom of the tin, on a high shelf, gas mark 7, until the fat is smoking hot.

Stir the batter mixture and pour into the hot fat. Put back in the oven for about fifteen minutes or until risen and brown.

Beef casserole with Dumplings

RT. HON. CHARLES KENNEDY MP

Serves 4

Casserole
2lb stewing steak, cubed
1oz seasoned flour
2oz butter
1 large onion, finely chopped
2 pints beef stock
1 bay leaf
$1/4$ pint soured cream

Dumplings
8oz fresh bread crumbs
4 tablespoons water
3 eggs, beaten
$1\frac{1}{2}$ tablespoons chopped parsley
1 onion, finely chopped

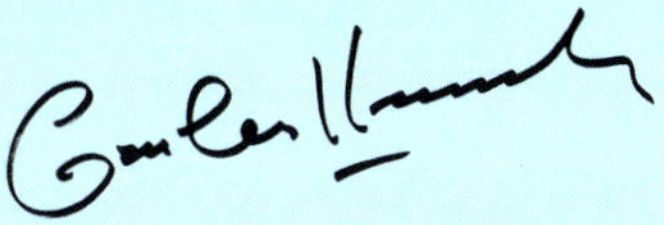

Pre-heat oven to 170°C/325°F/gas mark 3.

Coat beef cubes in seasoned flour. Melt butter in flameproof casserole dish. Add beef cubes to butter and brown on all sides. As cubes brown, remove from casserole, add onion to casserole and fry until softened.
Return beef to casserole. Stir in stock and add bay leaf.
Bring to boil, cover and transfer to oven. Cook for one and a half hours.

Whilst casserole is cooking, turn attention to dumplings.
Moisten breadcrumbs with water and mix in eggs. Season with salt and pepper to taste. Add parsley and mix together.
With floured hands, take mixture and mould dumplings.

After the initial one and a half hours is up . . .
Add dumplings to casserole. Spoon stock over ingredients. Recover casserole and continue cooking for a further half hour.
Remove bay leaf. Finally, spoon the sour cream over casserole before serving.

Pesto, Shrimp & Avocado Salad

JULIAN LENNON

Serves 1

a handful of shrimps
1 garlic clove, chopped finely
half teaspoon of balsamic vinegar
half ripe avocado chopped into small cubes
1 heaped tablespoon pesto sauce
(ready made is fine)
salt and pepper
juice of 1 lemon
fresh ginger, about the same amount as
the garlic when chopped
2 rounded tablespoons mayonnaise
(ready made is fine)
fresh chopped basil and shredded lettuce
for garnish

Put the shrimp in the lemon juice, add the chopped garlic, chopped ginger, balsamic vinegar and the chopped avocado. Mix gently. Add a little salt and pepper if you wish. Marinate for at least half an hour. Meanwhile, mix together the mayonnaise and the pesto. When the shrimp is ready, gently mix the shrimp and avocado marinade with the mayo and pesto. Serve on a bed of shredded lettuce with a sprinkling of chopped fresh basil on top.

PS: I generally serve this with a fresh sliced baguette for soaking up the remainder of the sauce after the shrimp has disappeared!

Paella

GARY LINEKER

Serves 6

2 tablespoons oil
3 chicken joints - halved
1lb rice
1 teaspoon paprika
1 tablespoon fresh parsley
juice of half lemon
4oz cockles
1 onion, peeled and chopped
8oz squid rings
half teaspoon powdered saffron
2 tablespoons tomato purée
1 and a half pints chicken stock
1lb mussels - frozen on the half shell and defrosted
4oz whole prawns

Heat oil in large frying pan and cook onion and garlic until soft.

Add chicken pieces and cook for 5 minutes. Add squid rings and cook for 2 minutes, turning everything over.

Add rice and stir. Add saffron, paprika, tomato purée and parsley, then add stock and lemon juice.

Bring to the boil, then turn down to simmer.

Add mussels and cockles and cook for 20 minutes or until rice is tender.

10 minutes before end of cooking time add prawns.

Oriental Fruit Compote with Honey & Ginger Yoghurt

MAUREEN LIPMAN

4oz dried apricots
4oz dried figs
half teaspoon ground cinnamon
4oz kumquats, sliced
1 teaspoon rosewater
1 teaspoon orange zest
4oz dried californian prunes
2oz plump sultanas
4oz stoned semi-dried californian dates
4oz bottle morello cherries
juice of one orange
2oz roasted peeled almonds

For the yoghurt

half pint greek yoghurt
1 tablespoon clear orange blossom honey
2 tablespoons stem ginger, finely chopped

Put the apricots, prunes, figs and sultanas in a serving bowl, add the cinnamon, cover with water and place in the fridge for one day.

Add the dates, kumquats, cherries and rosewater. Pour over the orange juice and stir in the zest.

Flavour the yoghurt with the honey, stir in the chopped ginger and pour into a serving bowl.

Just before serving, sprinkle the roasted almonds over the compote.

Roasted Vegetable Salad

KEN LIVINGSTONE

Preparation time: 10 minutes **Cooking time: 45 minutes**

225g (8oz) aubergines
1 red pepper
225g (8oz) tomatoes
75ml (5 tablespoons) olive oil
1 lemon
350g (12oz) courgettes
1 yellow pepper
6 garlic cloves
rock salt and milled pepper

Pre-heat oven to 200°C/400°F/gas mark 6.

Cut the vegetables into large chunks, de-seed the red and yellow peppers. Halve the tomatoes. Peel the garlic cloves and place all the vegetables in a large roasting tin in a single layer. Sprinkle the olive oil over and season generously with plenty of rock salt.

Roast for about 45 minutes or until tender and well browned, turning once during cooking.

Cool for about 30 minutes in the tin and then squeeze lemon juice over to taste. Adjust seasoning. Lift the vegetables onto serving plates or into one large bowl. Serve straight away or leave to cool.

To make a complete meal, this salad can be served with slices of crusty bread. Rub each slice of bread with a clove of garlic. Toast slightly on both sides. Spread thickly with pesto sauce, then top with slices of mozzarella, emmenthal or goats cheese. Grill again until cheese just begins to melt.

Chocolate & Star Anise Mousse Cake

JAMES MARTIN

300g dark bitter chocolate (min. 60% cocoa fat)
6 eggs
50g caster sugar
100ml greek yoghurt
150g unsalted butter
1 1/2 teaspoon freshly ground star anise, sieved
4 bananas

Line the base and sides of a 20cm spring-bottomed cake tin with greaseproof paper and set the oven to 180°C. Melt the chocolate and butter in a metal bowl over a pan of simmering water.

Separate the eggs and whisk the yolks with the star anise and 2 tablespoons of the sugar for half a minute. Stir in the melted chocolate and mix well. Beat the egg whites with the remaining sugar until very stiff, quickly fold one-third of the whites into the chocolate mix, then gently fold in the remainder and pour the mix into the cake tin.

Place on the middle shelf of the oven and bake for 20 minutes. Remove from the oven and while it's cooling, peel the bananas and put them onto a small piece of tin foil. Add 10g of butter onto each banana and cook for about 5 minutes until golden brown. Remove from the grill and serve on a plate with a chunk of the chocolate cake and a spoonful of yoghurt for all those health conscious out there!

Pollo con Mascarpone e Limone

ENZO MAURO

(Chicken with Lemon and Mascarpone)

Serves 4

4 breasts of chicken
1 glass of white wine
250g mascarpone cheese
2 lemons
2 tablespoons olive oil
salt and black pepper

Slowly pan fry the chicken breasts in cooking oil. When cooked through, drain off the oil and season with salt and black pepper. Add the juice from the two lemons, the olive oil and the glass of wine. Cook a while until slightly reduced.

Serve topped with a healthy spoonful of mascarpone and more freshly ground black pepper to taste.

This dish is complemented well by fresh spinach and sauteed potatoes.

Enzo Mauro
Proprietor, Mauro's Italian Restaurant

My Mum's Blackberry Purée

BRIAN MAY

This is something very simple, yet to me, even now that I am (nearly) grown-up, this is still the most delicious substance known to man. My mum made it like this.

First, pick the blackberries while they are at their best, in late summer. Only use the ones which are ready to be picked - these are black all over and come off the plant with only a gentle pull. Wear covering on the hands and arms - the bramble bushes are vicious! About 200 luscious fat berries is a good number to make enough purée for two luxury helpings, or to store in the fridge, to sip at for treats over a week or so.

Put the blackberries in a pan with a teaspoon of water to get them started and a couple or three tablespoons of sugar (this is where it gets naughty), though you can adjust this amount of sweetening to taste. Gently bring to boiling point, stirring with a wooden spoon which you don't mind getting stained dark purple! Turn the flame to low and keep stirring and squashing the berries until the liquid becomes an even paste - not longer than 5 minutes or so anyway, because vitamin C doesn't survive very long at 100°C.

Now, if you had a couple of freshly scrumped Bramley's cooking apples, they could have been chopped up and put in the pan with the berries, for a thicker texture, greater volume of resulting purée and an extra tang. But blackberries on their own give the purest flavour.

Remove the pan from the heat and pour into a metal sieve over a glass or china bowl. Use the wooden spoon to churn the paste around, squashing the juice through and leaving the seeds behind.

The pure red elixir can now be eaten or put in the fridge. It tastes really fabulous poured over ice cream, or the 'junket' my mum used to make (a kind of vanilla blancmange), or as a sauce for fresh fruits, or just spooned slowly into the mouth as a wicked pleasure. My daughter also enjoys the purée frozen into an iced lolly.

Warning - this stuff stains everything it touches - wear a napkin - and is very acidic - go gently if your stomach is sensitive. But the flavour . . . it's a killer . . . guaranteed to blast your tastebuds into space!

Tuna Pasta Surprise

MARTINE McCUTCHEON

Take a can of dolphin friendly tuna in brine, open and drain excess fluid.

Place in a bowl along with six spring onions, cleaned and diced, a tin of sweetcorn, a splash of vinegar and three large tablesponns of salad cream. Add salt and black pepper and mix together.

Boil some fresh pasta swirls until tender, drain and add the tuna mixture.

Mix all together, adding more salad cream if necessary.

Serve with crisp green salad, new boiled potatoes and fresh crusty bread.

Yummy!

love always
Martine McCutcheon ☆

Chocolate Surprise

The Rt. Revd. CHRISTOPHER MAYFIELD Bishop of Manchester

Serve 4 - 6

4oz margarine
2 eggs
1 oz cocoa
4 oz sugar
3 oz self raising flour

Cream the margarine and sugar together and add the eggs, one at a time, with a little of the flour. Sift the rest of the flour and cocoa together and fold it in. Put the mixture into a greased ovenproof dish.

Sauce
half a pint of hot water; 4oz soft brown sugar; 2 teaspoons cocoa

Stir the hot water, brown sugar and cocoa together and pour it over the sponge mixture.

Bake in the oven 375°F/ 190°C/gas mark 5 for about 30 minutes.

Serve hot with single cream or ice cream.

+Christopher

Creamy Chicken Linguine

PHILIP NEVILLE

Many thanks for your letter detailing your 10th anniversary celebrity cookbook. I have to admit, I'm not much use when it comes to the kitchen and can count the times I've made a cup of tea on one hand, let alone anything else! Therefore, it is a blessing that my wife, Julie, is exactly the opposite and a marvellous little chef. I have chosen a recipe of hers which is my absolute favourite pasta dish.

500g linguine
teaspoon of flour
225g sliced mushrooms
150ml chicken stock
teaspoon dried tarragon
4 x chicken breasts, diced
2-3 knobs of butter
150ml dry white wine
300ml double cream
grated parmesan for serving

Melt butter in large frying pan, add chicken and cook until crispy and golden.

Pour in the wine and cook for a minute or two.

Add the mushrooms, stock, cream, flour and tarragon and cook at a moderate heat for 15-20 minutes, constantly spooning the sauce over the chicken until thickened.

Meanwhile, cook the linguine *al dente* and drain well. Once done, toss in the pan with the rich sauce and then spoon into deep pasta bowls and sprinkle with the grated parmesan.

Serve with hot crusty baguettes. ***Delicious!***

Norfolk Pheasant

DUCHESS OF NORFOLK

1oz flaked almonds
2 tablespoons olive oil
1 jar redcurrant jelly
2oz sultanas or raisins
2 pheasants
half pint chicken stock
4 level teaspoons cornflour
grated rind and juice of 2 oranges

Heat oil in large casserole. Brown pheasants all over.

Add stock, jelly, rind, juice and raisins/sultanas to birds. Season well.

Bring to boil, then cover tightly and cook in oven at 150°C/300°F for one and a half to two hours.

Remove birds from pot and joint or carve.

Mix cornflour to smooth paste with 4 tablespoons water. Add to juices and bring to boil. Adjust seasoning and pour over pheasants. Garnish with toasted almonds.

Anne Norfolk

Macaroni Bake

TOM O'CONNOR

1 large onion (sliced)
1lb minced beef
1 beef stock cube
5oz grated cheese (cheddar)
half pint milk
2 tablespoons oil
8oz can tomatoes
6oz macaroni
3 eggs
salt and pepper

Sauté onion until tender. Add mince and brown well. Stir in tomatoes, sprinkle in stock cube, season and simmer for 15 minutes.

Cook macaroni in boiling, salted, water, drain and add to meat, together with half the cheese. Turn into a dish and press down well. Beat eggs and add to milk with remaining cheese. Pour over meat mixture and bake for 30-40 minutes (gas mark no.4) until set and golden brown on top.

Pasta Penne Pollo

EAMONN O'NEAL

Quantities to suit:

Pasta penne
courgettes
onion
tomato purée
florentina sauce (available from supermarkets)
assorted vegetables to taste
chicken pieces
black olives
mushrooms
celery
double cream

Cook chicken for about half an hour in the oven.

Mix the vegetables, cream and sauce in a large oven proof dish.

Cook for one hour in the oven (200°).

Add the chicken and pasta.

Cook for a further forty five minutes.

Serve with garlic bread and/or salad and a chilled glass of Pinot Grigio.

Broad Bean & Thyme Risotto

FIONA PHILLIPS

Serves 4

350g young broad beans shelled (1kg in their pods)
85g unsalted butter
285g risotto rice, arborio or carnaroliv
6 springs thyme
1 litre light vegetable stock
1 small onion, peeled and chopped
150ml white wine
60g freshly grated parmesan

For the thyme cream

2 heaped teaspoons chopped thyme
3 heaped dessertspoons crème fraîche

Bring a large pan of water to the boil and cook the beans (allow about 6 minutes for fresh ones). Cool under running water, skin and reserve them. Heat the stock to simmering point on the stove and keep it on a low heat while cooking the risotto.

Heat 50g of the butter in a heavy-bottomed pan and sweat the onion over a low heat until translucent and soft; it must not colour. Add the rice and cook for 1 to 2 minutes. Pour in the wine and continue to soak until the liquid has been absorbed. Add the thyme sprigs and start to pour in ladles of simmering stock - at no stage should the rice be flooded. It will take about 25 minutes to cook.

Stir in the parmesan and the remaining butter. Remove the thyme sprigs and add the beans to heat through. Adjust seasoning and serve with a spoonful of thyme cream in the centre.

Spaghetti with salmon + mushrooms . .

Simon Ratcliffe (Basement Jaxx)

Olive Oil
2/3 cloves garlic crushed
Mushrooms sliced
Pack of smoked salmon, cut into strips
200 g double cream
lemon juice.

Heat olive oil in a pan. Add garlic. Cook for 30 seconds. Add mushrooms + cook til brown + soft. Add salmon strips + leave for 30 seconds. Pour enough double cream to cover everything. Add lemon juice + some black pepper.

Cook spaghetti til al dente. Add some olive oil. Serve with green salad, french loaf + red wine . . .

Not very posh I'm afraid, but very good nosh. Hope it's okay.

Transkei Mud

Sir CLIFF RICHARD

Serves 8

Preparation time: 20 minutes
Cooking time: 2 hours, plus overnight cooling for condensed milk and overnight refrigeration for pudding

1 x 405g can condensed milk
200g digestive biscuits
284ml carton double cream
100g mint chocolate (such as aero), grated

Boil the can of condensed milk, unopened, and completely covered with water at all times, for about two hours. Allow it to cool fully, or overnight.

Whisk the double cream until it stands in soft peaks. Slowly add the caramelised milk, one spoonful at a time. Mix thoroughly.

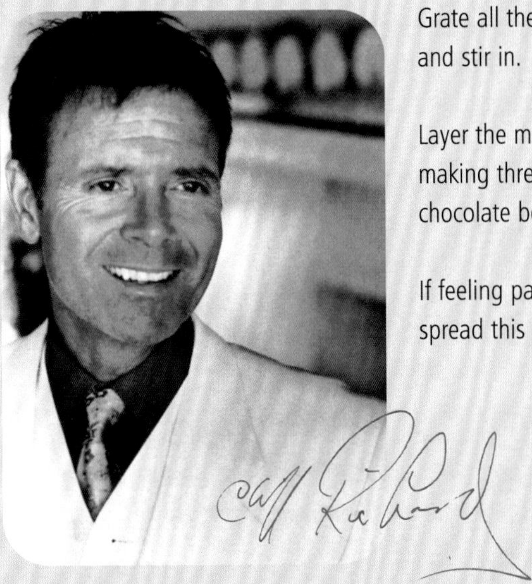

Grate all the chocolate, then, reserving a little for decoration, add it to the mixture and stir in.

Layer the mixture into a glass serving dish, alternating with the digestive biscuits, making three layers of each. Refrigerate overnight. Sprinkle over the remaining chocolate before serving.

If feeling particularly indulgent, whip a second carton of double cream until stiff and spread this over the pudding before decorating with remaining chocolate.

Serve in small portions as this pudding is very rich.

Barbecue Sauce

ADAM RICKITT

This recipe was handed down to me by my dad. I don't know where he got it from, I think he just sort of made it up! Anyway, we always have it with roast ham, but it's good with anything else - burgers, sausages, etc.

Hope you enjoy it as much as I do.

olive oil
3 large crushed cloves of garlic (or more to taste)
tomato tin full of white wine
2 large tablespoons hp sauce
2 large tablespoons worcestershire sauce
1 large tablespoon tomato purée
1 tablespoon mixed/italian herbs
2 small (1 large) onion
1 tin chopped tomatoes (plain or herbs and garlic)
3 large tablespoons of vinegar
1 large tablespoon tomato sauce
1 large tablespoon sugar
3 thick slices of lemon
2 heaped teaspoons cornflour

Soften onion (halved and thick sliced) and garlic in olive oil for 3-5 minutes on low heat.

Add all the rest of the ingredients. Bring to the boil. There will initially be a very frothy top, push that into the boiling bubbles and simmer for 20 minutes. Put on one side until needed.
Reheat gently, mix cornflour and water and add to the mixture, stirring constantly. Bring to the boil still stirring and simmer for one minute, stirring all the time.

Remove from heat and allow to cool.

Lemon Ice Cream

WILLIAM ROACHE MBE

8oz tub of whipping cream

8oz tube of Greek yoghurt

4-5 meringues (can be bought ready made)

1 jar of lemon curd or lemon syrup

Whip cream to a thick consistency and fold in yoghurt and flavouring (any flavouring can be substituted eg. strawberry syrup or maple are very nice). Break in meringues and beat them well, preferably with an electric blender as you don't want any lumps. Then freeze. It is simple and quick but very tasty with fruit and puddings or on its own. It is also good to take on picnics as it takes a long while to thaw.

You can also use it thawed as a rich cream.

Ragôut of Chicken & Mussels in a Basil & Aniseed Sauce

JOE ROYLE

Serves 4

25g (1oz) shallots, roughly chopped
1 tablespoon parsley stalks
1 litre (1.75 pint) fresh mussels, scraped and cleaned
150ml dry white wine
600ml (1 pint) chicken stock
olive oil
1 leek, finely diced
2 carrots, finely diced
1 stick of celery, finely diced
150ml (quarter pint) double cream
1 small fennel bulb, finely diced
1 clove garlic, crushed
1 tablespoon chopped thyme
1 bay leaf
3 tomatoes, skinned, seeded and diced
salt
freshly ground black pepper
4 x 175g (6oz) chicken breasts
5 tablespoons pernod or ricard

Lightly melt butter in pan, add the shallots and parsley stalks and place the mussels on top. Moisten with the white wine and half the chicken stock. Cover the pan, place it on a high heat and steam until the mussels open their shells about 1 minute. Pour the mussels into a colander, reserving the cooking liquid and discard any that do not open. Set aside.

In another pan heat together a little oil and butter, 'sweat' the vegetables, including the garlic, thyme, bay leaf and tomatoes for 2-3 minutes with the lid on. Remove the lid and place the seasoned chicken breasts on top. Moisten with the Pernod or Ricard, pour over the reserved mussel liquid and the remaining stock. Cover with buttered greaseproof paper and poach for 10-15 minutes, or until the chicken is tender.

Remove the chicken breasts and keep warm. Fish out and discard the bay leaf. Boil the sauce rapidly to reduce, add the double cream and whisk in a few small pieces of butter to give a rich smooth sauce.

Cut the chicken into small escalopes or thin slices and arrange on a warmed serving dish. Add the mussels to the sauce and reheat them without boiling. Check the seasoning, add the basil leaves and pour the sauce over the chicken.

Serve immediately.

Fried Oysters

JOHN SAVIDENT

Serves 4 - 6 as a starter

2-3 dozen oysters
milk
cornmeal, biscuit crumbs or fresh breadcrumbs
1/4 pint olive oil
2 eggs, beaten
salt and freshly ground black pepper
1/4lb butter
lemon wedges

Shell oysters.

Combine beaten eggs and a little milk in a bowl. Season to taste with the salt and pepper. Dip oysters in egg mixture, then in cornmeal or crumbs and allow to set on foil for about 5 minutes before cooking.

Melt butter in a large thick-bottomed frying pan. Add olive oil; bring to frying heat and cook oysters until golden brown. Serve immediately with wedges of lemon.

Banoffee Pie

CAROL SMILLIE

Serves 12

Large packet of digestive biscuits
1/2 teaspoon dried ginger
10-12 bananas
2oz caster sugar
1/2lb melted unsalted butter
1 tin condensed milk (see below)
1 1/2 pints of double cream
1oz dark chocolate

Boil the unopened tin of condensed milk in a pan of water for two and a half hours and leave to cool down for at least 6 hours before opening.
NOTE: Do not allow to boil dry as the tin will explode.

Place biscuits into a robo chef and grind until crumbed, add dried ginger and then slowly add melted butter.

Place the mixture into a loose bottomed flan dish and allow to set in the fridge for approximately half an hour.

Open the tin of condensed milk carefully. This will be set. Now spread onto the base.

Slice bananas onto this using as many or as little as you like.

Whip up the double cream with the caster sugar and pipe all over the bananas.

Grate the dark chocolate over the cream and put in the fridge until ready to serve. Enjoy!

Preserved Ginger Cake with Lemon Icing

DELIA SMITH

Makes 15 squares

5 pieces preserved stem ginger in syrup, chopped
1 heaped teaspoon ground ginger
6oz (175g) butter, at room temperature, plus a little extra for greasing
1 tablespoon molasses syrup
1 tablespoon ground almonds
2 tablespoons ginger syrup (from jar of stem ginger)
1 heaped teaspoon grated fresh root ginger
6oz (175g) golden caster sugar
3 large eggs, at room temperature
8oz (225g) self raising flour
2 tablespoons milk

For the topping
juice 1 lemon; 8oz (225g) unrefined golden icing sugar; 2 extra pieces preserved stem ginger in syrup

You will also need a non-stick cake tin measuring 6x10 inches (15x25.5cm), 1 inch (2.5cm) deep, and some silicone paper (parchment) measuring 10x14 inches (25.5x35cm). Pre-heat oven to gas mark 3/325°F/170°C.

First, prepare the cake tin by greasing it lightly and lining it with the silicone paper: press it into the tin, folding the corners in to make it fit neatly - the paper should come up 1 inch (2.5cm) above the edge.

To make the cake, take a large mixing bowl and cream the butter and sugar together until light and fluffy. Next, break the eggs into a jug and beat them with a fork until fluffy, then gradually beat them into the mixture, a little at a time, until all the egg is incorporated. Next, fold in the ginger syrup and molasses; the best way to add the molasses is to lightly grease a tablespoon, then take a tablespoon of molasses and just push it off the spoon with a rubber spatula into the mixture. Now sift the flour and ground ginger onto a plate, then gradually fold these in, about a tablespoon at a time. Next, fold in the almonds, followed by the milk and lastly the grated root ginger and pieces of stem ginger. Now, spread the cake mixture evenly in the cake tin, then bake in the middle shelf of the oven for 45-50 minutes, or until the cake is risen, springy and firm to touch in the centre. Leave the cake to cool in the tin for 10 minutes, then turn it out onto a wire rack and make sure it is absolutely cold before you attempt to ice it.

For the icing, sift the icing sugar into a bowl and mix with enough of the lemon juice to make the consistency of thick cream - you might not need all the lemon juice. Now, spread the icing over the top of the cake, and don't worry if it dribbles down the sides in places, as this looks quite attractive. Cut the remaining ginger into 15 chunks and place these in lines across the cake so that when you cut it you will have 15 squares, each with a piece of ginger in the centre. It's absolute heaven. If you'd like one or two of these cakes tucked away for a rainy day, they freeze beautifully - simply defrost and put the icing on half an hour before serving.

Thai Risotto with Aubergine

PENNY SMITH

Serves 4   Preparation time: 25 minutes   Cooking: 30 minutes

Creamy rice, flavoured with lemon grass, ginger, chilli and coconut milk - simply heavenly!

75g (3oz) butter
1 clove garlic, crushed
1 red chilli, deseeded and chopped
1 teaspoon freshly chopped root ginger
1 aubergine, cut into 12 mm/half inch chunks
100ml (3½fl oz) dry white
200ml (7 fl oz) unsweetened coconut milk
100g (4oz) shiitake mushrooms, wiped and sliced
3 sliced spring onions and fresh coconut shavings to garnish
1 onion, peeled and chopped
2 sticks lemon grass
half teaspoon curry powder
200g (7oz) pumpkin, cut into 12mm/half inch chunks (optional)
250g (9oz) arborio (risotto) rice
900ml (one and a half pints) hot vegetable stock
1 tablespoon freshly chopped mint
banana or vine leaves (optional)

Melt half the butter in a heavy based pan, add the onion, garlic, lemon grass, chilli, curry powder and ginger, cook gently for 3-4 minutes, stirring occasionally, until tender. Add pumpkin, aubergine and rice and cook for a further 1 minute. Add the wine and a little of the stock and cook, stirring occasionally, until the liquid has been absorbed into the rice.

Repeat this process with the remaining stock for about 25 minutes until the rice is tender but firm to the bite - towards the end of the cooking time, add the stock in smaller quantities. Keep checking to see if the rice is cooked. You may have some stock left over.

Add coconut milk and mint, then stir. The consistency of the risotto should be fairly loose. Season, set aside and cover to keep warm.

Melt remaining butter in a pan, add mushrooms and cook for 4 minutes until golden. Arrange risotto on banana leaves, top with mushrooms, garnish and serve with fruit chutney or chilli soy dip.

Spaghetti Aglio e Oglio

ED STEWART

Serves 4

This is one of my favourite recipes as cooked by my wife Chiara.

10 tablespoons olive oil
salt
ground black pepper or chilli
2 cloves garlic, finely chopped
500g spaghetti
small bunch chopped parsley

Cook spaghetti in normal way.

While it is cooking, put oil, garlic and salt in a small pan and sauté over very low heat, stirring until it becomes golden.

When pasta is cooked (al dente), drain and transfer to warm bowl and add oil and garlic, pepper and parsley and mix - add more olive oil if you like.

Lemon Yoghurt with Blueberries

UNA STUBBS

Serves 4

2 cups (16 fl oz) thick plain yoghurt
1 tablespoon very finely grated lemon rind
2 teaspoons gelatine
1/4 cup icing sugar, sifted
3/4 cup (6 fl oz) cream
6 1/2oz blueberries

Place the yoghurt, sugar and lemon rind in a bowl and mix to combine. Allow to stand until the mixture reaches room temperature.

Place the cream in a saucepan over low heat and heat until hot. Sprinkle with the gelatine and stir for two minutes until the gelatine is dissolved. Add the cream and gelatine mix to the yoghurt and stir to combine.

Place the blueberries into 4 3/4 cup ramekins or moulds. Pour in cream and yoghurt mix and refrigerate for 3 hours or until firm. Serve with the remaining blueberries.

These are great for brunch or dessert.

Grilled Squid with Kiwi & Lime Marinade

CHRIS TARRANT

This is one of my favourite recipes for squid, as the kiwi juice makes the squid very sweet and tender . . . Hope you enjoy it!

Marinade

juice of a kiwi fruit
2 tablespoons olive oil
1 chopped red chilli (optional)
juice of half a lime
1 clove garlic, crushed
salt and black pepper

Ask the fishmonger to clean the squid, removing the intestines and pen. Wash and skin the tentacles if used.

Cut the body open to give a large triangle of flesh. With a sharp knife, scrape the membrane from the inside of the fish, turning it over to scrape off any skin or membrane from the other side.

Using a sharp knife, make diagonal cuts across the flesh at about half inch intervals - do not cut right through the squid. Do this both ways to give a cross-hatched appearance.

Mix the marinade ingredients together.

Cut the squid into serving-size portions and cover with the marinade. Leave for 30 minutes, then cook under a hot grill for 3-4 minutes a side.

I like to serve this with sauté potatoes and a rocket salad.

Calvados Pheasants

The Rt. Hon. The Baroness MARGARET THATCHER LG OM FRS

1 brace pheasants, jointed
1.5oz (40g) butter
10 shallots, peeled
herbes de Provence
8oz mushrooms
10fl oz (275ml) calvados
10fl oz (275ml) stock
12oz (350g) streaky bacon
2 cloves garlic, chopped
2 bay leaves
10fl oz (275ml) dry white wine

Season joints, fry in butter and oil until golden brown. Transfer to casserole.

Fry shallots in remaining fat, remove to plate.

Chop bacon and fry.

Add herbs, bay leaves and garlic to pheasant. Add stock, wine and calvados. Bring to simmer, cover and cook for 45 minutes.

Add mushrooms, bacon and shallots. Simmer for further 45 minutes.

Remove pheasants to pre-heated dish.

Boil sauce, reduce, thicken. Pour sauce over the pheasant and serve.

Peach Melba Crumble

PAULA TILBROOK

4oz organic wholemeal flour
2oz ground almonds
3oz soft dark brown sugar
2 tins sliced peaches in fruit juice
Chopped nuts to taste
2oz organic porridge oats
3oz butter or low fat cooking margarine
4oz raspberries
a little extra sugar for top

(If using fresh peaches, you will need about 6 skinned, stoned and sliced. Depending on availability, fresh or frozen raspberries can be used.)

Mix the flour, oats and ground almonds together in a bowl and rub in the fat to crumb consistency. Add the sugar to the mixture. Place to one side.

Prepare fruit. Raspberries - if frozen, allow to thaw. Put peaches in a large oven to table dish with some of the juice. Place the raspberries over the peaches and then cover the fruit with the prepared crumble mixture.

Top with a little brown sugar and sprinkle with chopped nuts to give it a crunchy texture.

Cook in oven 350°F/180°C or gas mark 4 for approx. 30 minutes.

This delightfully crunchy and satisfying crumble tastes all the better if made with as many organic ingredients as possible.

Enjoy.

Paula Tilbrook

Lamb Cutlets Shrewsbury

ALAN TITCHMARSH

Serves 4

Time taken: 2 hours

8 lamb cutlets
4 oz button mushrooms
2 tablespoons worcester sauce
1 level tablespoon plain flour
salt and freshly ground pepper
chopped parsley
½ oz vegetable fat
4 tablespoons redcurrant jelly
juice of 1 lemon
quarter-half pint stock
pinch ground nutmeg

Trim excess fat from cutlets. Heat fat in frying pan, brown cutlets on both sides in hot fat. Trim and slice mushrooms.

Remove cutlets from pan and place in casserole dish with mushrooms.

Measure redcurrant jelly, worcester sauce and lemon juice into a saucepan. Stir over low heat until jelly has melted and ingredients are blended. (Stirring with a whisk often helps redcurrant jelly to soften.) Draw off the heat.

Add flour to hot fat remaining in frying pan and if necessary, add extra to help absorb the flour. Stir over low heat for about 10 minutes until a golden brown. Stir in jelly mix and then sufficient stock to make a thick gravy. Bring to boil stirring all the time to get smooth. Season with salt, pepper and nutmeg. Strain over cutlets.

Cover and place in a moderate to slow oven (325°F/170°C/gas 3) and cook for one and a half hours.

Sprinkle with parsley and serve.

Eton Mess

PHIL VICKERY

4 - 6 portions **Preparation time: 15 minutes** **Cooking time: none**

4 meringues, crushed but not too small, meringues made with brown sugar are good as they add a nice caramel edge to the finished sweet
three quarters of a pint of double cream, very lightly whipped
1 tablespoon caster sugar
9oz strawberries, English are the best by far
1 fresh vanilla pod, split and the seeds removed or a few drops of vanilla extract
2 heaped tablespoons of icing sugar
juice of 1 large fresh lemon
2 roses with nice perfume

Pick the roses from the stalks and roughly chop, add the lemon juice and icing sugar and leave for one hour. Then liquidise or whisk well so you end up with a nice chunky purée.

Hull the strawberries and cut into quarters, sprinkle on the vanilla seeds or extract, caster sugar and leave for 15 minutes.

To serve, fold the strawberries into the cream, add the meringues and a little of the rose petal sauce. Do not overwork as the lemon juice will thicken the cream, so pop into glasses and serve straight away and as cold as possible.

It is essential that the cream is only lightly whipped or the dish will spoil.

Dutch Rice

CAROL VORDERMAN MBE

225g (8oz) rice
150g (6oz) bacon
1 heaped teaspoon marmite
1 large onion
2 eggs
2-3 tablespoons vegetable oil

Boil rice using the preferred method. Peel and slice onion, trim and chop the bacon and beat the two eggs. Dissolve the marmite in a cupful of boiling water and stir well.

Heat the oil in a large frying pan, add the sliced onion, fry gently, then remove from the pan. Next, fry bacon and return onion to pan. Pour beaten eggs over the mixture and allow eggs to cook slowly, stirring constantly. Keep adding cooked rice.

Finally, add the marmite bringing the mixture to the boil then down to simmer until excess moisture has evaporated.

Serve piping hot with soy sauce (if liked)

This recipe was given to my mother when she lived in Holland and it continues to be the favourite dish of all the Vordermans.

Smakelijk eten!

Seized Chicken Breast with Asparagus & Muscat Risotto

RYLAND WAKEHAM

Serves 4

Risotto

1/2oz butter
2 shallots, finely diced
7oz arborio rice
1 1/2 pints chicken stock
4 chicken breasts - skin on
1 tablespoon chopped chervil
2 tablespoons mascarpone cheese
1 tablespoon olive oil
2 cloves garlic, chopped
1 glass sweet white wine
5oz asparagus chopped/cooked
2 tomatoes - flesh diced
1 tablespoon chopped chives

Heat butter and oil, sauté shallots and garlic (no colour). Stir in rice and cook for 2 minutes. Add wine and cook to absorb. Add stock to risotto a little at a time. Stop at this point - check seasoning.

Batten out chicken breast a little, season and pan roast for 3-5 minutes on each side.

Heat risotto and stir in asparagus, tomato concasse, herbs and mascarpone. Put risotto in an egg ring in centre of plate. Cut each chicken breast into 2/3 slices and arrange on top. Drizzle basil pesto around and parmesan shavings on top of chicken.

Basil Pesto Drizzle (You can buy this if wish to cheat!)

2oz grated parmesan
2oz parsley
1oz pine nuts
8 fl oz olive oil
2oz basil leaves
2 cloves garlic chopped
few walnuts
salt and pepper to taste

Place all ingredients except oil in a food processor and chop up.
Slowly add oil and check seasoning.

This may look a daunting recipe but well worth the effort.

R.J. Wakeham

The White House,
Prestbury

Pan Fried Smoked Salmon with Avocado

LESLEY WATERS

Serves 4

4 tablespoons olive oil
2 plum tomatoes, skinned, deseeded, and thinly sliced
juice of half lemon
1 large ripe avocado, halved, stoned, peeled and sliced
225g (8oz) smoked salmon slices
1 bunch chives, roughly chopped
1 bag mixed salad leaves
salt and freshly ground black pepper

In a non-stick frying pan, heat 1 tablespoon olive oil. Add the smoked salmon pieces, grind over some black pepper and fry for 2-3 minutes.

Meanwhile, heat the remaining oil in a small saucepan. Add the plum tomatoes, chives and a good squeeze of lemon juice. Season and gently heat through.

Arrange the salad leaves on four serving plates. Top with the avocado slices. Arranged the cooked smoked salmon pieces, slightly folded on the avocado and spoon over the hot tomato and chive dressing.

Serve at once.

Fillets of Trout Pan-fried with Rosemary & Smoked Bacon

ROSEMARY WATTS & MATTHEW BARRETT

Served with a Port and Red Wine Butter Sauce

Serves 4

4 fillets of trout (skinned and boned)
3 shallots (sliced)
1 tablespoon brown sugar
250g piece smoked bacon (cut into thick lardons)
6 cherry tomatoes
2 sprigs rosemary
salt, pepper and a little flour

1/4 pint red wine and ruby port
1 clove garlic (peeled and sliced)
80g butter
1 tablespoon double cream
4 sprigs chervil
1 sprig thyme

Coat the trout fillets in seasoned flour. Warm a little butter in a frying pan. Fold fillets in half and fry with rosemary on a medium heat until golden brown. Finish cooking in the oven for approximately 5 minutes.

For the sauce

Melt a little butter in a saucepan and fry shallots, garlic, rosemary and thyme for 5 minutes on a medium heat. Add brown sugar, red wine, port and bring to the boil, then simmer until reduced by half.
Add the cream, bring back to the boil, whisking all the time. Gradually add the butter to the sauce until a nice consistency is established (be careful not to boil sauce too much).

Fry the bacon lardons and drain on kitchen paper. Cut cherry tomatoes in half and arrange three pieces with bacon alternately around the plate. Strain sauce through a fine sieve and pour onto plates. Place fish in the centre and garnish top with chervil.

Chicken Consommé with Tarragon and Quails Eggs

DUCHESS OF WESTMINSTER

Serves 6

3 pints good chicken stock
8oz onion (one whole onion)
1 chicken carcass or the equivalent in bones
3 quails eggs per person
8oz mixed vegetables
4 egg whites
fresh tarragon

Place the stock in a thick bottomed pan and whisk in the egg whites.

Add the mixed vegetables (diced) to the stock, the fresh tarragon and the chicken carcass or bones.

Wash the onion and trim the root, leaving the skin on, cut in half and burn, cut side down, on the hot plate, add to the stock (the burnt onion will add a warm amber colour to the soup).

Place on the hot plate and bring slowly to the boil, stirring occasionally. When boiling, stir once more then allow to simmer very gently for one hour. Strain through a muslin cloth. De-grease if necessary and correct seasoning.

Poach the quails eggs for a short time, then cool in cold water.

To serve, place 3 quails eggs (previously warmed in a small amount of consommé) into individual tureens and pour over the chicken consommé. Garnish with a very thin slice of lemon and one or two leaves of tarragon.

Pears in Coffee

JUNE WHITFIELD

Serves 6 - 8

4 large firm pears
half a pint (10 fl oz) made-up coffee
double cream
2oz (50g) demerara sugar
3 tablespoons tia maria

Peel, halve and core pears.

Place flat side down in ovenproof dish, sprinkle with sugar.

Preheat oven to 160°C/325°F/gas mark 3.

Pour on coffee and liqueur and cook, covered, for about 35 minutes until just tender. Do not overcook.

Cool, cover and store in fridge for up to one week.

Serve cold with lots of cream.

June Whitfield

Eggs Rita

(Named after Ann's mother!)

THE RT. HON. ANN WIDDECOMBE M.P.

Serves six people as a starter

Very lightly scramble four eggs.

Do not allow the mixture to set.

Add 2 teaspoons full of thick cream and 2 teaspoons of sherry.

Stir in well.

Allow mixture to set according to taste.

Delicious wrapped in smoked salmon or with asparagus.

Banana Cake

BOB WILSON

Makes 1kg (2lb) loaf   Cooking time: one and a half hours

225g (8oz) self raising flour
100g (4oz) butter or margarine
75g (6oz) raisins
half teaspoon vanilla essence
3 tablespoons milk
half teaspoon salt
175g (6oz) soft dark brown sugar
2 ripe bananas
1 egg, beaten

Preheat oven to 160°C/325°F/gas mark 3

Line the bottom of a 1kg (2lb) loaf tin with greaseproof paper and grease the tin all over.

Place the flour and salt in a bowl. Add the butter or margarine, cut into pieces and rub into the flour until the mixture resembles fine breadcrumbs.

Stir in the sugar and raisins. Mash the bananas, essence, beaten egg and milk. Beat until well mixed. Turn the mixture into the prepared tin and smooth the top with the back of a spoon.

Place the tin on a baking sheet and bake in the oven for one hour and thirty minutes until the cake is golden brown and springs back when pressed with the fingers.

Leave in the tin for 10 minutes, then turn out and cool in a wire tray.
Serve sliced, either plain or buttered.

Cullen Skink

RICHARD WILSON

Serves 4 as a main course, 8 as a starter

Poach about 2lb of smoked haddock and a large chopped onion in a little water. When tender remove the skin and bones from the fish and flake it. Return to the pan, add one and half pints of milk and bring to the boil. Then add about half a pound of mashed potato (or more if you want the soup thicker) and stir to creamy consistency. Cut two ounces of butter into small pieces and add to the soup. Season to taste and add a little cream before serving.

Best wishes Richard Wilson

Caviar Pie

TERRY WOGAN

You will need a $9^{1}/_{2}$" loose bottomed flan dish, and the following ingredients . . .

6 hard boiled eggs (shelled)
Salt and fresh ground black pepper
3 x 2oz (50g) jars of lumpfish caviar
2oz (50g) butter
2 tablespoons finely chopped spring onions or chives
2 x 5fl oz (130ml) cartons of soured cream

Put the eggs, butter and some pepper into a blender or processor and blend until smooth. Taste and season well, then spread this mixture into the base of the flan dish, cover and chill for about three hours.

About half an hour before serving, spread the lumpfish caviar evenly over the eggs and sprinkle with a tablespoon of spring onions (or chives).

Now, spread the soured cream in a broad band around the edge, leaving a centre circle, showing the lumpfish caviar underneath. Sprinkle with remaining onions (or chives) and chill until ready to serve.

Remove the outer circle of the flan dish without disturbing the base and serve the pie on the flan base, transferring to a serving dish and cut into wedges.

This is delicious served with smoked salmon - Irish salmon of course!

Carrot Cake with Cream Cheese Frosting

ANTONY WORRALL THOMPSON MOGB

Serves 6-8

450g (1lb) self-raising flour
half tablespoon ground cinnamon
half teaspoon allspice
225ml (8fl oz) olive oil
225g (8oz) cooked pureed carrots
115g (4oz) chopped walnuts
55g (2oz) desiccated coconut
2 teaspoon baking powder
half teaspoon grated nutmeg
225g (8oz) soft dark brown sugar
3 large free range eggs, lightly beaten
115g (4oz) shredded carrot
115g (4oz) raisins
55g (2oz) tinned crushed pineapple, drained

Pre-heat oven to 180°C/350°F/gas mark 5.
Layer a 9" spring-form tin with buttered greaseproof paper.

Sift together flour, baking powder, cinnamon, nutmeg, allspice.
Fold in brown sugar and combine well.

Add the oil, eggs, carrot puree, carrot, walnuts, raisins, coconut and pineapple.

Pour the mixture into the lined tin (some may prefer the more traditional loaf tin).
Place in the oven and bake until the edges pull away from the sides of the pan and a skewer inserted in the centre comes out clean.

Cool the cake in the tin for 15 minutes, then unmould onto a cake rack, remove waxed paper and allow to cool. Frost the top and sides with the cream cheese mix (see below).

Cream Cheese Frosting

In a food processor, blend together 125g ($4^1/_2$ oz) cream cheese or Mascarpone with 250g (9oz) icing sugar, 90g ($3^1/_2$ oz) unsalted butter, half a teaspoon vanilla essence and juice of half a lemon until smooth.

Chicken Escalope in Cajun Mustard Sauce

PAUL YOUNG

The nut coating on the chicken is a nice touch that I stole from my old keyboard player, Ian Kewley. The sauce is so easy; just throw it all into a pan! Here goes:

4 chicken breasts
nut roast mix (from any health food store)
olive oil
breadcrumbs (not golden)
2 or 3 eggs

Sauce

half cup of double cream
6 tablespoons wholegrain mustard
1.5 teaspoons french mustard
quarter teaspoon black pepper
eighth teaspoon red (cayenne) pepper
half cup of sour cream
2 teaspoons worcester sauce
half teaspoon salt
quarter teaspoon white pepper
eighth teaspoon dried basil

First, batter the chicken breasts into a flat escalope, crack the eggs and whisk into a shallow dish. Also, pour a 50/50 mix of the breadcrumbs and the nut roast mix into another shallow dish and mix together.

Pre-heat your oven to a medium heat (gas mark 6, is that about 425°?). Pour a couple of tablespoons of oil into a frying pan over a medium heat. Dip the chicken breasts first into the egg mixture (that's the glue!), then in the bread/nut mix so that the breasts are evenly coated in the nuts and breadcrumbs. Then fry the breasts in the frying pan for about 5 minutes each side, taking care not to burn the nutty coating. Check that the breasts are just cooked with a fork and a sharp knife. Place the breasts on an oven tray and place in the centre of the oven to finish off while you prepare the sauce.

As I said, place all the ingredients in a small saucepan over a medium heat and turn to a low setting as soon as it begins to bubble. Simmer and stir for 15-20 minutes then turn off the heat. Sauces are much better if they're not too hot.

Place the chicken breast on a warm plate and spoon the sauce over the top.

Best accompaniments: steamed carrots or butternut squash, with fried courgettes (in a little oil and salt). Oh, go on, have a baked potato if you want to!

Enjoy!

FRANCIS HOUSE CHILDRENS HOSPICE
0161
434 4118